BAPTISTWAY

Bible Study for Texas

MW01124253

Good News in the New Testament

Duane Brooks

Ebbie Smith

Bill Tillman

BAPTISTWAY PRESS®
Dallas, Texas

Good News in the New Testament—Study Guide

Copyright © 2001 by BAPTISTWAY PRESS®.
All rights reserved.
Printed in the United States of America.

No part of this book may be used or reproduced in any manner whatsoever without written permission except in the case of brief quotations. For information, contact BAPTISTWAY PRESS, Baptist General Convention of Texas, 333 North Washington, Dallas, TX 75246–1798.

BAPTISTWAY PRESS® is registered in U.S. Patent and Trademark Office.

Scripture marked NIV is taken from The Holy Bible, New International Version (North American Edition), copyright © 1973, 1978, 1984 by the International Bible Society. Used by permission of Zondervan Publishing House.
Unless otherwise indicated, all Scripture quotations
in Unit 1 are from the New International Version.

Scripture marked NRSV is taken from the New Revised Standard Version Bible, copyright 1989, Division of Christian Education of the
National Council of the Churches of Christ in the United States of America.
Used by permission. All rights reserved.
Unless otherwise indicated, all Scripture quotations
in Units 2 and 3 are from the New Revised Standard Version Bible.

Scripture marked NASB is taken from the New American Standard Bible®,
Copyright © The Lockman Foundation 1960, 1962, 1963, 1968, 1971, 1972, 1973, 1975, 1977, 1995. Used by permission.

BAPTISTWAY PRESS® Management Team
Executive Director, Baptist General Convention of Texas: Charles Wade
Coordinator, Church Health and Growth Section: H. Lynn Eckeberger
Director, Bible Study/Discipleship Center: Bernard M. Spooner

Publishing consultant: Ross West, Positive Difference Communications
Cover and Interior Design and Production: Desktop Miracles, Inc.
Front cover photo: David M. Cochran

First edition: September 2001.
ISBN: 1–931060–12–6

How to Make the Best Use of This Issue

Whether you're the teacher or a student—

1. Start early in the week before your class meets.
2. Overview the study. Look at the table of contents, read the study introduction, and read the unit introduction for the lesson you're about to study. Try to see how each lesson relates to the unit and overall study of which it is a part.
3. Use your Bible to read and consider prayerfully the Scripture passages for the lesson. (You'll see that each writer has chosen a favorite translation for each unit in this issue. You're free to use the Bible translation you prefer and compare it with the translation chosen for that unit, of course.)
4. After reading all the Scripture passages in your Bible, then read the writer's comments. The comments are intended to be an aid to your study of the Bible.
5. Read the small articles—"sidebars"—in each lesson. They are intended to provide additional, enrichment information and inspiration and to encourage thought and application.
6. Try to answer for yourself the questions included in each lesson. They're intended to encourage further thought and application, and they can also be used in the class session itself.

If you're the teacher—

A. Do all of the things just mentioned, of course.
B. In the first session of the study, briefly overview the study by identifying with your class the date on which each lesson will be studied. Lead your class to write the date in the table of contents on page 5 and on the first page of each lesson. You might also find it helpful to make and post a chart that indicates the date on which each lesson will be studied.

C. You may want to get the enrichment teaching help that is provided in the *Baptist Standard* and/or on the internet. Call 214–630–4571 to begin your subscription to the *Baptist Standard*. Access the internet information by checking the *Baptist Standard* website at http://www.baptiststandard.com. (Other class participants may find this information helpful, too.)

D. Get a copy of the *Teaching Guide*, which is a companion piece to these lesson comments. It contains additional Bible comments plus teaching suggestions. The teaching suggestions in the *Teaching Guide* are intended to provide practical, easy-to-use teaching suggestions that will work in your class.

E. After you've studied the Bible passage, the lesson comments, and other material, use the teaching suggestions in the *Teaching Guide* to help you develop your plan for leading your class in studying each lesson.

F. Enjoy leading your class in discovering the meaning of the Scripture passages and in applying these passages to their lives.

Good News in the New Testament

UNIT 3

Interpreting the Meaning of Jesus

Good News in the New Testament

This series of thirteen lessons presents the opportunity to overcome a persistent shortcoming that many adults have, including many people who have been studying the Bible "all their lives." Even long-time Sunday School members may have just a smattering of knowledge about the New Testament—a story here, a teaching there, a half-remembered idea about something Paul wrote. These adults may not see, however, how it all fits together. This series of studies can help adults overcome this inadequacy and develop an understanding of the New Testament as a whole.

These thirteen lessons provide a brief survey of the New Testament. Lessons deal with various New Testament books, and the various kinds of writings in the New Testament are treated in the study. These writings include the gospels, Acts, letters, and the Book of Revelation. The focus of the study is, simply, Jesus, who is the focus of the New Testament itself.

The first unit, "The Ministry of Jesus," deals with the ministry of Jesus as seen in the four gospels. The first three lessons of this four-session unit are from the Gospels of Matthew, Mark, and Luke. The emphasis in these first three lessons is on the dominant theme of Jesus' ministry—Jesus' proclamation and embodiment of the kingdom of God. The first lesson, from the Gospel of Mark, deals with the beginning of Jesus' ministry, when he came announcing, "The time is fulfilled, and the kingdom of God is at hand; repent and believe in the gospel" (Mark 1:15, NASB). This lesson is placed first because of the widespread consensus among Bible commentators that Mark was the first gospel written. The second lesson, from the Gospel of Matthew, is a study of the kind of life that is lived under God's reign. The third lesson is a study of Luke 9:18–27 and calls for a decision about who Jesus is. The fourth lesson of the unit considers the climactic event of Jesus' ministry—his death and resurrection.

The second unit, "The Ministry of Jesus Continues," consists of three lessons from the Book of Acts. These lessons will lead participants to consider how Jesus continued his ministry in the actions of the early church.

The lessons will also challenge participants to consider how Jesus yet continues his ministry in *our* lives and churches. The first lesson points out that Acts 1:1 refers to an earlier writing, the Gospel of Luke, as being about "all that Jesus began to do and teach" (NIV, NASB). The implication is that Acts shows what Jesus continued to do and teach. This lesson considers Jesus' promise that the Holy Spirit would come upon the disciples and empower them to witness. The second lesson considers also how the early church proclaimed the message of Christ. The third lesson deals with the Jerusalem council, at which the church affirmed that salvation is indeed by grace through faith.

The third unit, "Interpreting the Meaning of Jesus," treats the remainder of the New Testament—the letters, Hebrews, and the Revelation. This six-session unit deals with six key themes of the New Testament—the meaning of the new life in Christ, our ministry for Christ, the meaning of faith, the necessity of love for one another to demonstrate the genuineness of our relationship to God, the promised coming of Christ, and the wonder of Jesus' redemptive work on our behalf.

Additional Resources for Studying *Good News in the New Testament* (arranged in canonical order)[1]

Joe Blair. *Introducing the New Testament*. Nashville: Broadman Press, 1994.

David E. Garland. *Reading Matthew: A Literary and Theological Commentary on the First Gospel*. New York: Crossroad, 1995.

Frank Stagg. *Matthew*. The Broadman Bible Commentary. Volume 8. Nashville: Broadman Press, 1969.

James A. Brooks. *Mark*. The New American Commentary. Volume 23. Nashville: Broadman Press, 1991.

David E. Garland. *Mark*. The NIV Application Commentary. Grand Rapids, Michigan: Zondervan Publishing House, 1996.

R. Alan Culpepper. *The Gospel of Luke*. The New Interpreter's Bible. Volume IX. Nashville: Abingdon Press, 1995.

Malcolm Tolbert. *Luke*. The Broadman Bible Commentary. Volume 9. Nashville: Broadman Press, 1970.

George R. Beasley-Murray. *John*. Word Biblical Commentary. Volume 36. Waco, Texas: Word Books, Publisher, 1987.

William E. Hull. *John*. The Broadman Bible Commentary. Volume 9. Nashville: Broadman Press, 1970.

William Barclay. *The Acts of the Apostles*, The Daily Study Bible Series. Revised edition. Philadelphia: The Westminster Press, 1976.

J. W. MacGorman. *Acts: The Gospel for All People.* Nashville, Tennessee: Convention Press, 1990.

I. Howard Marshall. *The Acts of the Apostles: An Introduction and Commentary.* Tyndale New Testament Commentaries. Grand Rapids, Michigan: William B. Eerdmans Publishing Company, 1987.

John B. Polhill. *Acts.* The New American Commentary. Volume 26. Nashville, Tennessee: Broadman Press, 1992.

Smith, T. C. *Acts.* The Broadman Bible Commentary. Volume 10. Nashville, Tennessee: Broadman Press, 1970.

William Barclay. *The Letter to the Romans.* The Daily Study Bible. Philadelphia: The Westminster Press, 1975.

G. R. Beasley-Murray. *2 Corinthians.* The Broadman Bible Commentary. Volume 11. Nashville: Broadman Press, 1971.

Kenneth L. Chafin. *1, 2 Corinthians.* The Communicator's Commentary. Volume 7. Waco, Texas: Word Books, Publisher, 1985.

David E. Garland. *2 Corinthians.* The New American Commentary. Volume 29. Nashville: Broadman and Holman, 1999.

Fred B. Craddock. *The Letter to the Hebrews.* The New Interpreter's Bible. Volume XII. Nashville: Abingdon Press, 1998.

Foy Valentine. *Hebrews, James, 1 and 2 Peter.* Layman's Bible Book Commentary. Volume 23. Nashville, Tennessee: Broadman Press, 1981.

William Barclay. *The Letters of John and Jude.* The Daily Study Bible. Philadelphia: The Westminster Press, 1976.

Pheme Perkins. *First and Second Peter, James, and Jude.* Interpretation: A Commentary for Teaching and Preaching, (Louisville: John Knox Press, 1995).

Ray Summers. *2 Peter.* The Broadman Bible Commentary. Volume 12. Nashville: Broadman Press, 1972.

Herschel H. Hobbs. *The Cosmic Drama: An Exposition of the Book of Revelation.* Waco, Texas: Word Books, Publisher, 1971.

M. Eugene Boring. *Revelation.* Interpretation: A Commentary for Teaching and Preaching. Louisville: John Knox Press, 1989.

John P. Newport. *The Lion and the Lamb.* Nashville, Tennessee: Broadman Press, 1986.

Ray Summers. *Worthy Is the Lamb: An Interpretation of Revelation.* Nashville, Tennessee: Broadman Press, 1971.

NOTES

1. Listing a book does not imply full agreement by the writers or BAPTISTWAY PRESS® with all of its comments.

The Ministry of Jesus

This unit provides a brief summary of the ministry of Jesus as seen in the four gospels and consists of one lesson from each gospel. The first three lessons are from the Gospels of Mark, Matthew, and Luke.

These lessons focus on the dominant theme of Jesus' ministry—his proclamation and embodiment of the kingdom of God. The final lesson, from the Gospel of John, considers Jesus' resurrection and its meaning. A brief introduction to the gospel being studied is a part of each lesson.[1]

UNIT ONE, THE MINISTRY OF JESUS

NOTES

1. Unless otherwise indicated, all Scripture quotes in Unit 1, Lessons 1–4, are from the New International Version.

Focal Text

Mark 1:1–15

Background

Mark 1:1–15

Main Idea

Jesus proclaimed and embodied the kingdom of God.

Question to Explore

How does Jesus' ministry fit into God's purpose in history— and for my life?

Study Aim

To summarize how Jesus' ministry fits into God's purpose in history and for my life

Study and Action Emphases

- Share the gospel of Jesus Christ with all people
- Equip people for ministry in the church and in the world

LESSON ONE

It's Time

Quick Read

At just the right time in history, Jesus came proclaiming the good news of the kingdom of God as the fulfillment of prophecy and of John the Baptist's announcement of Jesus' ministry.

Do you ever catch yourself saying, "It's time"? Those words can mean a lot or a little, depending on the context. How do you know that it is time?

When my wife and I were viewing the sonogram of our first son, the technician took a look at the readout and asked, "When did you say you were due?"

We said, "Early in April."

He said, "Not according to this measurement. This baby is further along than you think."

We said, "Really?"

He said, "Yes, he will be born in early March, not in early April."

That whole conversation wouldn't have mattered if I hadn't received a phone call just the next week from a church inviting me to preach a week-long revival in late March. Based on the ultrasound, I now knew the baby would be about a month old. Without asking Melanie, I accepted the church's gracious invitation. Sure enough, the ultrasound was wrong. It was a long month of waiting, knowing the revival was coming and realizing that Melanie had not had the baby. March didn't really march. March dragged along, and we still had no baby.

When the time came to preach the revival, Melanie was 9.2 months pregnant. So I went to preach, and we stationed a church member by the phone at the church. I was out in a rural area sixty miles from our home. On Sunday morning, Melanie came with me to the meeting, but on Sunday night she was too tired. So I drove down by myself and preached. When I got home that night, as I walked in the door, she said, "It's time!"

If you think that pregnancy passes slowly, think about the world's wait for the awaited one to come. Since the fall of humankind, the world had been waiting, groaning in travail, crying out for redemption. The gestation period had dragged on for hundreds of years since Isaiah had spoken. People were waiting. And, as strange as it may sound, God had been waiting. Then, as Paul said in Galatians 4:4, "When the time had fully come, God sent his Son." In God's great plan for the ages, a day came when God looked down from heaven and said, *It's time.*

Then Jesus was born, his parents fled with him to Egypt, and then they moved to Nazareth. One day, John began to preach. Then Jesus came to be baptized and blessed. Shortly after that, Jesus began to preach. What did he say? *It's time!*

Who is Jesus? There are so many conflicting opinions about that subject. In the New Testament are four ancient witnesses who answer that question. Mark was likely the first to write. Mark begins with a declaration

Mark 1:1–15

¹The beginning of the gospel about Jesus Christ, the Son of God.
²It is written in Isaiah the prophet:
    "I will send my messenger ahead of you,
    who will prepare your way"—
³ "a voice of one calling in the desert,
  'Prepare the way for the Lord,
    make straight paths for him.'"

⁴And so John came, baptizing in the desert region and preaching a baptism of repentance for the forgiveness of sins. ⁵The whole Judean countryside and all the people of Jerusalem went out to him. Confessing their sins, they were baptized by him in the Jordan River. ⁶John wore clothing made of camel's hair, with a leather belt around his waist, and he ate locusts and wild honey. ⁷And this was his message: "After me will come one more powerful than I, the thongs of whose sandals I am not worthy to stoop down and untie. ⁸I baptize you with water, but he will baptize you with the Holy Spirit."

⁹At that time Jesus came from Nazareth in Galilee and was baptized by John in the Jordan. ¹⁰As Jesus was coming up out of the water, he saw heaven being torn open and the Spirit descending on him like a dove. ¹¹And a voice came from heaven: "You are my Son, whom I love; with you I am well pleased."

¹²At once the Spirit sent him out into the desert, ¹³and he was in the desert forty days, being tempted by Satan. He was with the wild animals, and angels attended him.

¹⁴After John was put in prison, Jesus went into Galilee, proclaiming the good news of God. ¹⁵"The time has come," he said. "The kingdom of God is near. Repent and believe the good news!"

of the timeliness of Jesus' coming. For 400 years, the prophetic voices had been silent. Then John the Baptist came on the scene saying, *It's almost time.* Mark 1:9 says, "At that time Jesus came," and in 1:15, Jesus announced, "The time has come." The time for what? The time for good news, for the beginning of Jesus' ministry, for the kingdom to come on earth as it was in heaven!

So exactly what time was it? In God's plan there was a time when Jesus came, and there is a time when Jesus will come again. So what time is it for those of who live in between those two comings? This is the time for us to come to him. At just the right time, the One who transcends time took the time to enter our time. How do we get ready? First we recognize that his coming is good news, and then we repent of sin and receive the Savior.

Today it is time for us to make time in our lives for him! Just as there was a time for God's Son to be born into this world, there is a time for us to be born into God's kingdom. Mark reminds us that we are living on KST—Kingdom Standard Time. Let's get ready and get right!

> In God's great plan for the ages, a day came when God looked down from heaven and said, It's time.

In the beginning of his gospel, Mark went directly to the heart of Jesus' ministry. Mark starts by relating Jesus to the fulfillment of the prophecies of Isaiah and John the Baptist. Then Mark shows us Jesus' emphasis on the proclamation of the kingdom of God from the first.

Good News: It's Time to Recognize His Coming (1:1–5, 15)

Are we ready for the good news of Christ's entry into our lives? From the beginning the prophets made it known that preparation would be required (see Malachi 3:1; Isaiah 40:3). Isaiah predicted that a messenger would come to prepare the way for the Lord. John the Baptist embodied the fulfillment of that prophecy. He came to prepare the way by preaching a simple message: *Get ready!*

Dr. George Sweeting, former President of Moody Bible Institute in Chicago, told of the day he noticed an unusual combination of bumper

The Gospel of Mark

The Gospel of Mark offers us the earliest and simplest account of Christ. In the famous words of Sergeant Friday on the television show *Dragnet*, Mark provides us "just the facts." Tradition tells us that Mark was written by John Mark, the companion of the Apostle Paul who defected during Paul's first missionary journey (Acts 15:36–40). Though Mark's desertion created conflict between Paul and Barnabas, the tension was ultimately resolved when Paul admitted how much he needed him (2 Timothy 4:11). Mark was apparently in Peter's company as Peter wrote his first letter (1 Peter 5:13). Many scholars believe that Mark wrote down the reflections of Peter, one of Jesus' inner circle of disciples. The Gospel of Mark likely was written after the middle of the first century in the city of Rome.

stickers on the car of a man who was visiting the school. The coincidental message conveyed by the two stickers prompted Dr. Sweeting to suggest to the unsuspecting visitor that he might want to remove one of them. One bumper sticker read, "Jesus Is Coming," and the other said, "Escape to Wisconsin."

The people of Jesus' day thought they were ready for the coming of the Messiah, but they largely missed it. Are we really

Who is Jesus?

ready? We need to stay ready so we don't have to get ready! Are we living as people who recognize Jesus' first coming and his impending second coming?

Some people live with a functional atheism. They aren't really atheists, but nothing in their work habits, family lives, or neighborhood relationships indicates to anybody that they really know the One who has come. What about you?

Good News: It's Time to Repent of Our Sins! (1:4–6, 15)

John the Baptist preached repentance and baptism so the people would get ready by forsaking their sin. His message attracted great crowds of people. They prepared for Christ's coming through repentance, which literally means changing their minds, and through confession, which means admitting their sins. Once they took the step of repentance and confession, then they were ready for baptism, which symbolized the renewal they had experienced.

At just the right time, the One who transcends time took the time to enter our time.

Note in 1:15 that Jesus also preached the need for repentance. How can it be time for good news if we have to worry about sin? Acknowledgement of sin is actually very good news. When we have sinned, we can be forgiven if we acknowledge our sin. It is impossible for us to find release from our problems if they are all caused by abuse or mistreatment by somebody else. But, in repentance, we own our responsibility for our lives and accept God's complete healing and redemption.

Sometimes we are sorry that we have been caught in sin. The anguish of being caught is very painful indeed. But we should not mistake that for true repentance.

Repentance is not like the person who sent the IRS a check for $150 with the explanation, "I have cheated on my taxes and I can't sleep. Enclosed is a check for $150. If I still can't sleep, I'll send the rest."

Repentance involves a change of attitude and action. While my family vacationed in Glacier National Park one summer, the one thing we hoped not to do was encounter a bear. The closest we came was at the top of Logan Pass at the Continental Divide where we saw a group of hikers about a half-mile away walking across a snow pack. Suddenly, somebody yelled, "Bear!" After a quick visual search for the bear, we were convinced the message was true because the long line of hikers all turned and retraced their steps, walking in the opposite direction. Repentance requires more than being sorry for our sin. Genuine repentance means changing from the wrong direction to the right direction.

Mark reminds us that we are living on KST—Kingdom Standard Time.

When we hate sin with a passion, when we fear nothing except displeasing God, when we change our minds about sin, then we have repented. Repentance is not just saying we have sinned or even admitting we are sorry we have sinned. Repentance is not just saying we won't sin again. Repentance is a fundamental change of mind about sin. Repentance is an about-face that acknowledges that our sin is always wrong.

When we have sinned, we can be forgiven if we acknowledge our sin.

What sin is holding us back? Whatever it is, Hebrews 12:2 says, "Let us throw off everything that hinders and the sin that so easily entangles." Not only is it time to get ready, but since Christ has come, ready or not, it is time to get right!

Good News: It's Time to Receive the Good News that the King Has Come! (1:1, 7–15)

After John the Baptist preached the need for repentance, he proclaimed the coming of Christ. From the beginning, John the Baptist humbled himself by recognizing the superiority of Christ. While John baptized with water, he predicted that the Messiah would baptize people in the Holy Spirit.

On cue, Jesus fulfilled John's preaching as John had fulfilled Isaiah's prophecy. When John the Baptist baptized Jesus, the Holy Spirit descended

The Kingdom of God

Jesus came preaching the kingdom of God. The Gospel of Matthew uses a parallel term, the kingdom of heaven. What is the kingdom of God? Is it a place? Mark's use of kingdom of God reminds us that it is more than a place. When Jesus spoke about the nearness of the kingdom of God (Mark 1:15), he was not referring to a location.

The term *kingdom* was filled with political implications in the first-century world. Caesar reigned without rival in the Roman world. The Romans had brought commerce and civilization with their great road system. Unfortunately, they also brought political oppression. The people of Jesus' day awaited a political Messiah who would deliver them from Rome. But Jesus' later refusal to fight when the religious leaders came to capture and crucify him clarifies that he never intended a political kingdom (14:46–48).

So what did Jesus mean by kingdom of God? An equivalent expression might be "the kingship of God." The time was coming near for people to recognize that God was their king. Centuries before, at the end of the period of the judges, the people of Israel had clamored for a king like the other nations around them. In so doing, they had rejected God as their king. A review of the kings of Israel and Judah reveals their inadequacies. Since the time of the exile, the people had been subjected to foreign rulers who were even less worthy. Jesus offered a radical reversal of the people's poor choice about wanting a human king. What if God were King of the people again? If people recognized the authority of God again, they would discover a different kind of life.

The kingdom of God requires preparation. In another call to repentance, Jesus told the people that it would be better to pluck out an eye and enter the kingdom of God with one eye than to have two eyes and be thrown into hell (9:47).

The kingdom of God calls for the recognition of God's presence and work in the world as God's rightful domain. By contrasting the kingdom to hell and speaking of entering the kingdom, Jesus equated it with a place where God reigns without rival. While we might think of that place as a future heaven, Jesus announced that this kingdom comes wherever people receive it humbly, like little children (10:14).

on Jesus like a dove. God further confirmed Jesus as the Messiah with a voice of affirmation from heaven. Immediately, the Spirit directed Jesus to go into the desert for a time of temptation and preparation.

What is the best news you have ever heard? Do you remember the day the Iron Curtain fell? I remember growing up in West Germany and entering East Germany through Checkpoint Charlie to see the dismal,

Case Study

Some years ago when I was pastor of Pleasant Grove Baptist Church near Waco, I went with a visiting evangelist to call on a young man who had not accepted Christ. Although the young man was respected for his integrity in the cattle business, he had no room for Christ in his life.

The young man initially resisted our efforts and argued that it was not "time" for him to receive Christ. However, he came to the revival one night. During that service, he received the good news and repented of his sins. The prayers of the entire church were answered that night. His wife and others confirmed that his lifestyle changed radically that night.

Recently I returned to the church to preach in a funeral service. The people told me that this young man is one of the leaders of the church.

Can you think of someone for whom you can pray to receive the good news? Do you believe that Christ still radically changes lives? Has Christ changed your life?

---

desperate gray world across the fence. I shared the jubilation when the people on the other side of the fence were finally free. The wonderful news led me to celebrate!

Mark wrote in 1:9, "At that time. . . ." As John's ministry came to an end, Jesus' ministry began. John was imprisoned, and Jesus went from the wilderness back to Galilee, the area where he was raised (1:14). There Jesus preached the good news of God.

Genuine repentance means changing from the wrong direction to the right direction.

Pay close attention to Jesus' first sermon. Jesus said, "The time has come" (1:15). What time had come? Jesus proclaimed that the time had come for his ministry, and the time had come for people to come to know God personally! Jesus proclaimed the nearness of the kingdom.

In the Greek language in which our New Testament was written there were different words for time. *Chronos* spoke of consecutive time. The word appears in our word *chronological*. Mark used another word when he wrote, "The time has come," however (1:15). The word in 1:15 is not *chronos*, but *kairos*. *Kairos* speaks of a specific moment in time, an appointed time or opportunity. Using the same word, Paul wrote to the Ephesians (5:16, KJV) that they should be "redeeming the time," referring to *kairos*, not *chronos*.

Some people feel trapped by *chronos*—chronological time. Have you felt the pressure of time? Porris Wittel, a dock worker in Gillingham, England, hated his alarm clock for forty-seven years. For forty-seven years, early every morning his alarm clock jangled him awake. For forty-seven years he longed to ignore it, to shut it off. And for forty-seven years he submitted to the pressure of that clock. But on the day of his retirement he got his revenge. He took his alarm clock to work and flattened it in an eighty-ton hydraulic press. He said, "It was a lovely feeling."

What is the best news you have ever heard?

Even though we may feel pressured by chronological time, the moment of opportunity represented by *kairos* time still lies open to us. It is time for us to respond to Jesus' coming. How do we do it? In the same way that the people of Jesus' day did. We believe and receive by faith the good news that Jesus has come for us!

When we believe that Jesus is the Christ, the Son of God (1:1), then we repent of our sins and receive his gift of life. Though we are tempted to procrastinate, Jesus' words speak with a compelling urgency today. The time is now, or it might be never (see 2 Corinthians 6:2).

QUESTIONS

1. How has Christ's coming measurably affected your life? What do you need to do to prepare for Christ's second coming? Is there any sin from which you need to repent? Confess it and turn from it today.

2. In your personal ministry, is there some *kairos* moment you need to seize? What is God calling you to do? Is today the day you will begin to serve the Lord actively?

3. Have you received the good news of God's kingship in your life? What specific steps could you take to acknowledge Christ's lordship in your life? Are you submissive, "like a little child," to the reign of Christ in your life?

4. What are you doing to proclaim God's kingdom to the world? Are you inviting others into relationship with Jesus Christ? Write down the names of three people who need to know Christ and pray for them now.

Focal Text
Matthew 4:23—5:16

Background
Matthew 4:23—7:28

Main Idea
Jesus taught that living under God's rule means living in a new and different way.

Question to Explore
What sort of life does God really want me to live?

Study Aim
To evaluate my life in light of the design for life under God's rule that Jesus taught

Study and Action Emphases
- Share the gospel of Jesus Christ with all people
- Minister to human needs in the name of Jesus Christ
- Equip people for ministry in the church and in the world

LESSON TWO

This Is Really Living

Quick Read
At the beginning of his ministry, Jesus called a small group of followers to join him in his twofold ministry of touching and teaching. In the Sermon on the Mount, Jesus instilled his value system in them by providing them a primer on the abundant life of the kingdom of heaven.

Bob Reid has brought history to life for generations of students at Baylor University. One sleepy summer morning, I walked into class without having read my assignment. As far as we students knew, Bob Reid had never given a pop quiz, and so we had no fear. Suddenly he came through the door holding up a stack of quizzes to test us over the reading.

Professor Reid taught us about grace that day, though, because he offered us the opportunity to ask a few questions before the quiz. We scrambled for our books and began to stall by asking questions as we read feverishly. He answered questions for a few minutes and then offered us one last chance by suggesting some other questions we might ask. We wrote down the answers as we continued to ask questions through the better part of the hour. Finally, he held up the "quizzes" and turned them over to reveal blank sheets of paper. There had never been a quiz. But we learned history that day.

Do you remember your favorite teachers? What made them great? The movie *Mr. Holland's Opus* told of a frustrated composer who must make his living teaching music in high school. All the while, he hopes to write his masterpiece, his opus, but the demands of teaching deny him the opportunity. After years of teaching, he plans to retire. Before the day of his retirement, though, he is surprised with a reception in which all of his former students return to play his best work. Ultimately, the students embody his greatest work.

When God came into the world in the person of Jesus Christ, he invested his time in the lives of a small group of followers. For three years, he taught them. At the end of his life, he had not personally won any great prizes, and neither had he written down any of his words on paper. He wrote them on human hearts, entrusting his disciples to carry the word to the world.

After Jesus called a group of disciples to learn from him, then he began to teach, preach, and touch people in need. His words and works became the curriculum for a three-year crash course in ministry training. The hallmark of Jesus' ministry was his authority. When Jesus spoke of the kingdom of heaven, he had authority because he had just come from heaven and he had always been the King!

Touching and Teaching—with Authority (Matthew 4:23—5:2)

Nearly everybody acknowledges that Jesus was a teacher. What kind of teacher was he? Matthew tells us that he taught in the synagogues and

Matthew 4:23–25

23Jesus went throughout Galilee, teaching in their synagogues, preaching the good news of the kingdom, and healing every disease and sickness among the people. 24News about him spread all over Syria, and people brought to him all who were ill with various diseases, those suffering severe pain, the demon-possessed, those having seizures, and the paralyzed, and he healed them. 25Large crowds from Galilee, the Decapolis, Jerusalem, Judea and the region across the Jordan followed him.

Matthew 5:1–16

1Now when he saw the crowds, he went up on a mountainside and sat down. His disciples came to him, 2and he began to teach them, saying:

3 "Blessed are the poor in spirit,
    for theirs is the kingdom of heaven.
4 Blessed are those who mourn,
    for they will be comforted.
5 Blessed are the meek,
    for they will inherit the earth.
6 Blessed are those who hunger and thirst for righteousness,
    for they will be filled.
7 Blessed are the merciful,
    for they will be shown mercy.
8 Blessed are the pure in heart,
    for they will see God.
9 Blessed are the peacemakers,
    for they will be called sons of God.
10 Blessed are those who are persecuted because of righteousness,
    for theirs is the kingdom of heaven.

11"Blessed are you when people insult you, persecute you and falsely say all kinds of evil against you because of me. 12Rejoice and be glad, because great is your reward in heaven, for in the same way they persecuted the prophets who were before you.

13"You are the salt of the earth. But if the salt loses its saltiness, how can it be made salty again? It is no longer good for anything, except to be thrown out and trampled by men.

14"You are the light of the world. A city on a hill cannot be hidden. 15Neither do people light a lamp and put it under a bowl. Instead they put it on its stand, and it gives light to everyone in the house. 16In the same way, let your light shine before men, that they may see your good deeds and praise your Father in heaven.

preached the good news (Matthew 4:23—5:1). We have an example of Jesus' teaching ministry in Matthew 5—7. Note in Matthew 5:1 that when Jesus "saw the crowds, he went up on a mountainside and sat down." When the learners or disciples came, he began to teach them. Jesus' teaching ministry was inseparable from his touching ministry. So, in Jesus' teaching, he spoke with compassion for the poor in spirit, the mourners, the meek, the hungry for righteousness, the merciful, the pure in heart, the peacemakers, and the persecuted.

At the end of Jesus' sermon, we learn, "the crowds were amazed at his teaching because he taught as one who had authority and not as their teachers of the law" (7:28–29). The word for *authority* is the same word Jesus would use in Matthew 28:18–19 when he said, "All authority in heaven and on earth has been given to me. Therefore go and make disciples of all nations." Jesus had authority when he taught, and he invested this authority in his disciples to make more disciples.

At the beginning of Jesus' ministry, as his popularity grew, he called his disciples to himself so that he might teach them what it means to be a Christ-follower. He had called them to follow, and they obeyed by following him up the hill. There he taught them eight keys to true happiness.

The Gospel of Matthew

Have you ever wondered why we have four different gospels? When we read them, we discover that each of them enriches our understanding of who Jesus Christ is. Tradition tells us that Matthew wrote his gospel in latter part of the first century, perhaps in the 80s or 90s AD. As a former tax collector and a Jewish believer, Matthew set Jesus' life in the framework of Judaism.

We saw in the first lesson that Mark prefers action to dialogue. Matthew builds on Mark's foundation by showing us some of the great teachings of Jesus Christ. Because Matthew wrote as a Jewish believer to Jews, it was natural for him to portray Jesus as the Teacher-Messiah. We owe a debt to Matthew for his inclusion of many of the parables as well as the Great Commission.

Even more, we appreciate Matthew's careful record of the Sermon on the Mount. In these three chapters of the gospel, Matthew gives us the beatitudes, the Lord's prayer, and many of Jesus' greatest ethical teachings.

The Sermon on the Mount reveals to us the teaching heart of Christ. Without question, the eight beatitudes or statements of blessing remain the signature ethical teachings of Jesus' ministry. They answer the vital question, *How does a citizen of the kingdom of heaven live?*

These keys, the beatitudes, do not represent works that save us. On the contrary they show us eight characteristics of those who find true spiritual happiness and fulfillment as followers of Christ.

In each of the beatitudes, Jesus stated a principle or prerequisite, "Blessed are . . ." those who act in a certain manner. He then stated a promise. Jesus stated that those who fulfill the prerequisites receive the promises and so are "blessed." The Greek word for "blessed," *makarios*, means something like, "Oh, how wonderfully happy."

Life in the Kingdom of Heaven (5:3–16)

To a world searching for true happiness, Jesus' teachings offer great hope. The promises relate to life in the "kingdom of heaven." This phrase is the equivalent of "kingdom of God," which Mark and Luke use instead of "kingdom of heaven." As we noted in the first lesson, this kingdom does not refer primarily to a place or a time but rather to the rule of Christ in the lives of his followers. The kingdom of heaven comes in our lives when the King of heaven reigns without rival in our hearts.

When Jesus spoke of the kingdom of heaven, he had authority because he had just come from heaven and he had always been the King!

Beatitude #1. "Blessed are the poor in spirit" (5:3). "Poor in spirit" describes well those who had come out to Jesus. They were not the self-satisfied religious leaders; rather, they were the desperately poor people who were seeking God with all their hearts. To them, Jesus brought the kingship and reign of heaven. For the first time in history, they found reason to hope for heaven and happiness. We become poor in spirit when we recognize our emptiness apart from God and his love for our lives.

When I visited Harris County boot camp for juvenile offenders, I saw people who were incredibly open to the gospel. In large part, it was because they had nothing else. Everything had been taken away from them. Not all of them were the same, either. Although some of the young people came from underprivileged backgrounds, others had actually enjoyed good jobs and educational backgrounds before they fell in with the wrong crowd. But the circumstances of this detention camp reduced them to the same level: they were poor in spirit and open to the gospel. There is a happiness in dependence on God that the spiritually independent and self-satisfied never experience!

Notice the promise: "Theirs is the kingdom of heaven!" Jesus also said this of the persecuted (5:10). This phrase, "kingdom of heaven," is the heart of the Sermon on the Mount. In 5:20, the kingdom is present so that we can enter it. In 6:33, we are told to seek it first, so that all these things will be added to us! The kingdom of heaven is not just a place but a relationship with the King. Thus, in that sense, the kingdom is already ours; it is a present possession, not just a future hope!

> The kingdom of heaven comes in our lives when the King of heaven reigns without rival in our hearts.

Beatitude #2. "Blessed are those who mourn, for they will be comforted" (5:4). After Jesus announced the coming of the kingdom to the poor in spirit, he offered comfort to those who had taken the next step of mourning their sin. It is one thing to be poor in spirit but another to mourn and grieve over sin.

In 2 Corinthians 12:21, Paul used a form of this same Greek word translated "mourn" to describe his reaction of grief to sin in the church at Corinth. In the same way, Paul used a form of this word in 1 Corinthians 5:2 in calling for grief over sin.

When do we mourn? While there may be a great deal of mourning over the pain of losing loved ones or over the unfairness of life, there is not enough mourning over individual and community sin. Only those who mourn sin ever experience the happiness God's comfort brings. Conviction must precede comfort!

Beatitude #3. "Blessed are the meek, for they will inherit the earth" (Matt. 5:5). What a revolutionary teaching! To a world that thinks that the meek will be slaves and the powerful will reign, Jesus not only taught that the meek will inherit, but also he proved it by his own life. At Calvary, in meekness, he allowed the religious leaders and soldiers to take his life, so that he could rise again on the third day and prove that he was Lord over all. As he taught his disciples, he explained to them the blessedness of meekness.

> The kingdom of heaven is not just a place but a relationship with the King.

We must not confuse meekness with weakness. Jesus possessed all power and authority, but he said to his followers in Matthew 11:29, "I am meek and lowly in heart" (KJV). The Greek word for meekness means strength under control. This word was used of a wild stallion that had been ridden, broken, and brought under control.

So often we think that we must take what we want in this world. But Jesus teaches us a revolutionary subordination in which we submit ourselves to God and trust him to provide for us. When we are under God's control, then we find ourselves under God's blessing.

Beatitude #4. "Blessed are those who hunger and thirst for righteousness, for they will be filled" (Matt. 5:6). Jesus was speaking to people who knew what it was like to be truly hungry and thirsty. Jesus reminded them that life consisted of spiritual realities. As he had told Satan in the wilderness, "Man does not live on bread alone, but on every word that comes from the mouth of God!" (4:4)

In the first three beatitudes, Jesus calls upon us to recognize our emptiness. In the fourth, he shows us how to be filled. We all need to be filled with something. What will it be? We can be filled with food and drink, or we can be filled with the Holy Spirit of God who alone can produce righteousness within us. Only those who hunger for God and his righteousness are ever filled with him.

> *When we are under God's control, then we find ourselves under God's blessing.*

Notice that Jesus said the hungry and thirsty "will be filled" (5:6). Once again he spoke of certainty. That we will "be" filled suggests that only God can do it. We cannot fill ourselves spiritually; we are not self-sufficient. Like the qualities of being poor in spirit, mourning, and being meek, this one recognizes that we have needs that only God can fill. The good news is that God wants to fill us with himself. When God empties us of all we are, then he cleanses us and fills us with himself so that he may pour us out on a dry world. (See also Psalm 107:9; John 6:35.)

Beatitude #5. "Blessed are the merciful, for they will be shown mercy" (Matt. 5:7). Jesus frequently taught the rule of reciprocity in life. Whatever we sow we also reap. In the fifth beatitude, Jesus shows how our relationship with a merciful Father causes us to be a merciful family. Here among God's people, if nowhere else in the world, we receive mercy. What does mercy mean? If grace is getting what we do not deserve, mercy is failing to get what we do deserve. "Mercy" assumes need on the part of the one who receives it and resources adequate to meet the need on the part of the one who shows it.

We live in a world that is vitally interested in its rights. People frequently say, *I want justice.* Whether or not we realize it, justice is not what we really want or need. We need mercy because all of us have gone astray.

The story is told that one winter's night in 1935, the mayor of New York, Fiorello La Guardia, showed up at a night court in the poorest ward of the city. The mayor dismissed the judge for the evening and took over the bench. That night a tattered old woman charged with stealing a loaf of bread was brought before him. She defended herself by saying, "My daughter's husband has deserted her. She is sick, and her children are starving."

"She must be punished to teach other people a lesson," said the shopkeeper.

La Guardia sighed. He turned to the old woman and said, "I have to punish you; the law makes no exceptions. Ten dollars or ten days in jail." While he was pronouncing the sentence, La Guardia reached into his pocket, took out a ten dollar bill and threw it into his hat with these famous words: "Here's the ten dollar fine, which I now remit, and furthermore I'm going to fine everyone in the courtroom fifty cents for living in a town where a person has to steal bread so that her grandchildren can eat." Forty-seven dollars and fifty cents was turned over to a bewildered old grandmother who had stolen a loaf of bread to feed her starving grandchildren.

> If grace is getting what we do not deserve, mercy is failing to get what we do deserve.

There came a time when the King of heaven left his throne, took off his crown, laid down his scepter, and came down here to us. When he saw our sin, he said, *The price must be paid. Blood must be shed for forgiveness to come.* But he paid it all by himself. He didn't take up a collection, but he shed his own blood. He had mercy. Have we ever come to know God as the God of mercy? If we do not know God as a merciful God, we do not really know him. Furthermore, we who wish to receive mercy must show mercy.

> Happiness belongs to those who live under the Lordship of Jesus Christ and experience the cleansing power of Calvary.

Beatitude #6. "Blessed are the pure in heart, for they will see God" (5:8). Who is happy? According to the advertisements, those who fill their lives with uncleanness and impurity are the happiest people of all. *Not so!* said Jesus. Happiness belongs to those who live under the Lordship of Jesus Christ and experience the cleansing power of Calvary. Jesus said the pure in heart will find happiness because they will see God. This purity of heart is not an accomplishment or a work that we perform by trying harder. Rather, purity of heart is a result of Christ's kingship over our lives. When Christ becomes the Lord of our lives, he

Claiming Christ's Promises

I've never seen a deacon friend of mine let circumstances, however extreme, rattle him. Alvin is the direct descendant of a Czech family in central Texas and is a gentle giant. Fifteen years ago, when a really big hurricane hit Texas, I was staying at his home. While I was sleeping, the hurricane spun off tornadoes in that area. The noise of tree limbs clattering against the window awakened me.

After the storm passed, we were sitting at the table eating a meal, and we could smell gasoline and diesel. My friend went out to see what had happened. He returned in a few moments and continued to eat. The conversation continued. After the meal, I said, "Everything was OK out there?"

He said, "No. A tornado touched down and wiped out the barn. It also turned over the fuel tanks."

In spite of the situation, though, he was visibly unaffected. A year or so later, he lost a finger in an accident at work. Yet in all of these events, I never saw him frazzled. In church business meetings, he was always in control. Whatever his net worth, he already has inherited the earth! How does the promise of our inheritance help you in times of loss and difficulty?

makes us clean by his power. God's work of sanctification transforms our lives into a perpetual purity.

Who are the pure in heart? The word translated "pure" is the word for *cleansed* that gives us our word *catharsis*.

Jesus did not speak of those who were ritually or ceremonially pure like the Pharisees. In fact he said that the righteousness of his disciples must exceed that of the Pharisees. The only way we can ever be pure in heart is to accept the cleansing of Christ and to abide in that.

Why are the pure in heart so happy? They will see God. What does this mean? Will we see him visibly? In this life and beyond, we will see God as we discern the presence and purpose of Jesus Christ for our lives.

Beatitude #7. "Blessed are the peacemakers, for they will be called sons of God" (Matt. 5:9). Nobody ever made peace like Jesus did. Paul wrote about Jesus in Ephesians 2:14, "He himself is our peace." No wonder Jesus told his disciples that when they made peace they would become sons and daughters of God and would experience great blessing and happiness. We are most like the Son of God when we make peace between people and God and between people and people. By making peace we confirm our relationship with God, and we claim God's promise of blessing and happiness.

31

The word *peace* has such a rich religious history. For the Jews, the word for *peace* was *shalom*, a word that meant not only the absence of strife but also the presence of all of God's goodness and gifts in our lives. To the religious leaders of Jesus' day, a peacemaker was a person who established right relationships with other people. Jesus lived in an era called the *pax Romana*, the peace of Rome. In theory, it was a time of great peace because nobody could conquer the Romans. It was not, however, a time of true peace. There was still political conflict. The zealots wanted to overthrow the Roman government's rule over Israel. There was religious conflict. The Pharisees and Sadducees could not get along with each other, much less with the Prince of Peace. All of these conflicts stemmed from the spiritual problem of not being at peace with God.

> We are most like the Son of God when we make peace between people and God and between people and people.

We have ongoing battles in our hearts and in our homes. We are most like the Son of God when we make peace between people and God and between people and people. Jesus even made peace with those who crucified him. Hebrews 12:14 says we are to "make every effort to live in peace with all men." Romans 12:18 says we are to "live at peace with everyone." When we forgive we confirm our relationship with the Heavenly Father and claim our joy. Peace is a distinctive of Christianity.

Beatitude #8. "Blessed are those who are persecuted because of righteousness, for theirs is the kingdom of heaven" (Matt. 5:10). With these words, Jesus brought the beatitudes full circle. The blessings are about those who surrender to the rule of the King of heaven and receive his kingdom in their lives. If we keep the first seven beatitudes, we will likely get to experience the eighth. In the eighth and final blessing Jesus pronounced, he blessed the persecuted with the promise of joy in the kingdom of heaven. In addition, Jesus said we are in the good company of the prophets who likewise suffered for their faith (5:11–12).

Early believers were insulted, persecuted, and even martyred. These early believers suffered for the sake of righteousness and for the sake of Christ. They suffered for the right reasons. What about today? Missiologists agree on this: More people have been martyred for the cause of Christ in the twentieth century than in the previous nineteen centuries combined. Our political and religious freedoms insulate us from these concerns in America, but Christ still calls us to be faithful to him, even though persecution might result.

Jesus' Call to Us (5:13–16)

Jesus taught his disciples that they were to be salt and light in the world. They were to live openly as Christians, making a difference for Christ, not shrinking into the woodwork or "going along to get along." That goes for us, too.

QUESTIONS

1. How will you use the authority of Christ to touch people around you who are hurting?

2. A number of anger-related accidents occur on our highways each year. Sociologists describe this phenomenon as "road rage." How can we show the meekness of Christ in our relationships with others, including how we drive?

3. Which three of the beatitudes are most difficult for you to practice?

Focal Text

Luke 9:18–27

Background

Luke 9:18–27

Main Idea

Jesus calls for a life-changing decision about what we believe about him.

Questions to Explore

Who do you really think Jesus was—and is?
What difference does it make in your life?

Study Aim

To confess faith in Jesus as God's Messiah

Study and Action Emphases

- Share the gospel of Jesus Christ with all people
- Equip people for ministry in the church and in the world

LESSON THREE

Who Is He?

Quick Read

Our answer to the question about the identity of Christ determines both our direction in life and our eternal destiny.

While I was in Waco for a meeting of the Baylor University Board of Regents, I entered an elevator with Dr. Howard Batson, pastor of First Baptist Church, Amarillo, and we stood on either side of the elevator. The next time the elevator stopped, two men entered the elevator. I thought one of the men looked familiar, even famous. As he was exiting the elevator, I asked him, "Are you who I think you are?"

The man turned and answered in a rich bass voice, "Yes. The name is Jones. James Earl Jones."

It was really James Earl Jones. Anyone who has ever listened to CNN has heard that rich, deep voice. I assure you that his voice is even better in person! As James Earl Jones walked away, Dr. Batson and I laughed at my question.

In Jesus' day many people were asking that question of him: *Are you who we think you are?* Two thousand years later, scholars and people from around the world are still asking, *Who is Jesus, really?*

In Luke 9:18–27, we discover that Jesus knew exactly who he was. It is one thing to know who we are, and another to deal with what people believe about us. Jesus handled these matters with prayer. Alone with God he found the strength he needed to prepare for what lay ahead. When Jesus' disciples approached him, he asked (Luke 9:18), "Who do the crowds say I am?" At this point great crowds had been following him, because they sensed the hand of God on Jesus as a prophet, but they did not know Jesus as the disciples did. The disciples had come to comprehend Jesus' true identity. He is the Christ—the Anointed One, the Messiah, who has come from God. In the verses that follow, Jesus identified himself as the Son of Man and invited the disciples to abandon everything in order to follow him. Had Jesus been just a teacher or a prophet, he could not have asked such a high price. If Jesus is who he says he is, then all of life is changed.

Our decision about who Jesus is will inevitably determine both our direction in this life and our destination in eternity. If Jesus Christ were just a man or even a great prophet, then we could pay him tribute on a parallel level with any number of other great historical teachers. But if we believe what Peter said (9:20), then we must abandon all for the sake of the call.

To follow Christ is to deny ourselves, take up our crosses, and follow him. Today, we must determine once and for all who we believe Jesus is. Who is Jesus to you? When we decide who, then we will know what to do!

Luke 9:18–27

¹⁸Once when Jesus was praying in private and his disciples were with him, he asked them, "Who do the crowds say I am?"

¹⁹They replied, "Some say John the Baptist; others say Elijah; and still others, that one of the prophets of long ago has come back to life."

²⁰"But what about you?" he asked. "Who do you say I am?"

Peter answered, "The Christ of God."

²¹Jesus strictly warned them not to tell this to anyone. ²²And he said, "The Son of Man must suffer many things and be rejected by the elders, chief priests and teachers of the law, and he must be killed and on the third day be raised to life."

²³Then he said to them all: "If anyone would come after me, he must deny himself and take up his cross daily and follow me. ²⁴For whoever wants to save his life will lose it, but whoever loses his life for me will save it. ²⁵What good is it for a man to gain the whole world, and yet lose or forfeit his very self? ²⁶If anyone is ashamed of me and my words, the Son of Man will be ashamed of him when he comes in his glory and in the glory of the Father and of the holy angels. ²⁷I tell you the truth, some who are standing here will not taste death before they see the kingdom of God."

Discovering Jesus' Identity (9:18–22)

Jesus invited his disciples to consider his identity. He used three questions to help them focus their thoughts and answers.

1. Who were people saying Jesus was (9:18–19)? Some people said Jesus was John the Baptist. Others said he was Elijah. Still others said that one of the prophets of long ago had come back to life. People recognized Jesus' dignity but not his deity. They understood him as a prophet speaking for God but not as the perfect Son of God.

Has anybody ever mistaken your identity? The actor Cary Grant once told how he was walking along a street and met a fellow whose eyes locked onto him with excitement. The man said, "Wait a minute, you're—you're—I know who you are. Don't tell me—you're Rock Hud . . . No, you're. . . ." Grant thought he'd help him, and so he finished the man's sentence: "Cary Grant." And the fellow said, "No, that's not it! You're. . . ." Cary Grant was trying to tell him who he was, but the fellow had someone else in mind.

In his sequel to this gospel, Luke wrote in Acts 4:12, "There is no other name under heaven given to men by which we must be saved!" The people represented one set of opinions about Jesus identity. The disciples offered another!

2. Who do disciples say Jesus is (9:20)? When Jesus asked the disciples who they said he was, Peter answered, "The Christ of God." To say that he was of God was to say that he had come from God or more specifically that he was God's Son. As the name "O'Brien" means "of Brien," implying direct descent, so Peter was asserting Jesus' descent from God.

3. Who did Jesus know he was (9:21–22)? Jesus took over at this point and began to define his messiahship on behalf of his disciples. He would not settle to become just a popular Messiah but a powerful one. He had not come to live as a celebrity but to die as a sacrifice for sins. Notice how Jesus defined his messiahship.

Two thousand years later, scholars and people from around the world are still asking, Who is Jesus, really?

First, Jesus denied the disciples the right to tell everyone he was the Christ, not because he doubted it, but because he doubted that the world was ready to receive it. This aspect of Jesus' teaching, frequently called the "Messianic secret," must not be interpreted as a denial of Jesus' messiahship. Jesus waited for the opportune moment to reveal this truth to the disbelieving religious leaders. These leaders were looking for ammunition to use against Jesus. By restricting the flow of this information, Jesus delayed the crucifixion until the time of God's choice.

Second, Jesus defined this messiahship in terms of suffering, rejection, crucifixion, and resurrection. In 9:51, Jesus resolutely set his face toward Jerusalem. He had no place to lay his head. He was ready to proclaim and

The Gospel of Luke

From the Book of Acts and Paul's writings we know that Luke was a physician who accompanied Paul on his missionary journeys. In the prologue of the Gospel of Luke, found in 1:1–4, Luke gave a clear explanation of his purpose in writing this gospel.

Luke offers us a wonderful portrait of Jesus' compassion for the outcasts and downtrodden of the world. His gospel contains more detail than Mark's simpler portrait and addresses an audience more Gentile than Matthew's apparently Jewish audience.

Many scholars date Luke's Gospel in the mid 70s AD.

ordain the kingdom of God! Jesus was not headed to the Jerusalem Hilton but to the cross!

Jesus knew exactly who he was. Remember that his Father spoke to him at the time of his baptism. When Peter called him the Christ, Jesus did not deny it, but he defined his messiahship in terms of being a suffering Servant.

It's time to stop being wimps as Christians.

The title, "Son of Man," also is significant. Is this just a title of humility to downplay his divinity? No. Luke 9:26 shows us that this title is an exalted title that is derived from the Old Testament description of the Messiah coming in power and great glory. (See Daniel 7:13–14.)

Jesus knew who he was! Who do we say Jesus is? If he is the Son of Man and the Son of God, then he is uniquely worthy of the devotion of our lives.

Discerning His Intention and Walking a Different Direction to a Different Destination (9:23–27)

Our comprehension of Jesus' identity determines our conduct and direction. Note what Jesus said: "If anyone would come after me, he must deny himself and take up his cross daily and follow me" (Luke 9:23).

The definition of true discipleship is self-renunciation. Jesus gave up heaven, and he gave up his life. What will we give up to follow him? Peter and John and James left their father and their fishing. What will we give up?

Our decision about who Jesus is will inevitably determine both our direction in this life and our destination in eternity.

One of my favorite pastimes is watching Baylor University play football. "Why?" you may ask. I suppose because I was at Baylor in 1980 when we were undefeated in the conference and went to the Cotton Bowl with a 10–1 record. I keep hoping (in vain, as of this writing) that it may happen again.

With our church's new Saturday night service, I realized that I would not be able to go to any of the games. When I was writing these lessons, I realized that the first game of the season would be on Thursday night. I was elated. Come what may, I determined I would be at that game. Then my little brother called and said, "Duane, we have a pre-wedding party this Thursday night. Can you come?"

"Taste Death"?

Who will not "taste death" before they see the kingdom of God? In Luke 9:27, Jesus implied that some of his disciples would see the kingdom of God before they died. What did he mean? Scholars offer a number of opinions about what Jesus was referring to, including these possibilities: the transfiguration, the crucifixion, the resurrection, the ascension, Pentecost, or the second coming.

In context, relating the prediction to the transfiguration makes a lot of sense. Jesus showed a small number of disciples the brightness of his presence when he was transfigured before them (9:28–36). In this experience they had the rare opportunity to see Moses and Elijah as well as to hear the voice of God affirming Jesus.

In the larger context of Luke, Jesus may well have been pointing not just to his transfiguration but to his resurrection. In Luke 24:13–32, he revealed the story of the resurrection to two followers on the road to Emmaus. Later, in 24:36–49, he appeared to the eleven disciples and revealed his resurrection.

Likely it is impossible to know precisely what Jesus meant in 9:27 apart from further information that is not available to us.

I had seen the invitation, but I told him, "No, I will be at the football game."

Then guilt began to gnaw at me as my wife suggested that I reconsider. When he called back later in the week, he asked, "Are you going to the football game?"

I answered, "No, I'm going to your party."

He said, "Duane, I can't believe you are giving up your only Baylor football game all year for me."

As brothers sometimes do, I capitalized on the opportunity to try to bring great guilt into his life. I said, "This is not just my only opportunity this year. In twenty years, Baylor has played every game I can remember on a Saturday. I plan to do Saturday night worship for the rest of my ministry. That means for the rest of my life I will never see a Baylor game live, and I am giving up this one chance for my little brother's pre-wedding party."

If Jesus is who he says he is, then all of life is changed.

Actually, Baylor football is not such a major concession to make. But is there anything you just won't give up for Jesus Christ? Whatever it is will keep you from becoming a true disciple of Jesus Christ. If we want to save our lives, we will lose them. But if we lose them here, we will gain them for life eternal!

The missionary to the Auca Indians, Jim Elliott once said, "He is not a fool who gives up that which he cannot keep to gain that which he cannot lose!"

As we think about taking up the cross ourselves, we must not confuse the cross with some physical ailment we struggle with or some character flaw we are struggling to overcome. The cross was a symbol of death, not an ornament to wear around one's neck.

Today, we must determine once and for all who we believe Jesus is.

To wear a cross in the first century would have been the equivalent of wearing a noose around one's neck today. We do not see the electric chair or lethal injection as a symbol of honor. The cross was the most brutal form of capital punishment. Jesus was asking would-be disciples whether they would be willing to die with him.

Case Study

At the 100th anniversary of the arrival of missionaries in Zaire, Christians gathered to celebrate from that part of Zaire once called the Belgian Congo. The festivities lasted all day, with music, preaching, food, and conversations. Many reminisced about the early days and praised God for the progress of the gospel and the church.

Near the end of the long program, a very old man stood to give a speech. He said that he soon would die and that he needed to tell something that no one else knew. If he didn't tell, his secret would go with him to his grave. He explained that when the first white missionaries came, his people didn't know whether to believe their message or not. So they devised a plan to slowly and secretly poison the missionaries and watch them die.

One by one, children and adults became ill, died, and were buried. It was when his people saw how these missionaries died that they decided to believe their message. Think of it—those missionaries never knew what was happening. They didn't know they were being poisoned, and they didn't know why they were dying. They didn't know they were martyrs. They stayed and died because they trusted Jesus. And it was the way they died that taught others how to live.

Would the sacrifice you are making lead others to see Christ in you? Are you becoming more like Christ in "the fellowship of sharing in his sufferings" (Philippians 3:10)?

A patient at a dentist's office tried to lighten her fear by listing her name on the registry as "The Wimp." A little later the receptionist stepped into the waiting room and said, "The doctor will now see the wimp." Four people stood up simultaneously.

Our comprehension of Jesus' identity determines our conduct and direction.

It's time to stop being wimps as Christians. The call of Christ to his disciples then and now is to be willing to die for him. In some countries of our world, believers are paying that price today. For those of us who live in a country with great religious freedom, the call is to live for him, sacrificing our ambitions and agendas for the sake of Christ's. Certainly Jesus wanted his disciples to know that he must become more important to them than their lives (9:24), the whole world (9:25), or their reputations (9:26). Our decision about the identity of Christ determines our eternal destiny. If we believe he is the crucified Christ, then we join him in a life of sacrifice and obedience.

We see this principle illustrated in the movie, *Spartacus*. In the movie, Spartacus was a slave who led a revolt against the Roman Empire. When they captured him and his troops, they were determined to crucify him, but they didn't want to kill all of his men. So they simply asked the men to identify him and let him be crucified. The rest of the men then would be allowed to live. But the inexplicable happened. Instead of turning against their leader, they all stood with him, claiming to be Spartacus. The movie ends with the Judean hillside dotted with innumerable crosses. They wouldn't let him die alone!

As Jesus' disciples, we must follow him—all the way to the cross. Are you willing to take up your cross? Now? How?

QUESTIONS

1. People still have various opinions about who Jesus is. What are some prominent views today? How do you respond to those views?

2. Why do you think Jesus told the disciples not to share their information about his identity? Why should we respond differently today?

3. Consider Peter's response to Jesus as recorded in Matthew 16:22–23. In what way does it clarify Jesus teaching in Luke 9:23–24? How does the world respond to the story of a suffering Savior today? How do you respond to Jesus' willingness to die?

4. How do you respond to Jesus' call for self-denial? What have you given up for the sake of following Christ? List some things you would give up for Christ's sake.

5. Spend a few moments meditating on the titles of Christ in this passage. Consider Jesus as the Christ and as the Son of Man. If Jesus is the Christ and the Son of Man, how should we respond to him?

Study Aim

To describe the significance for my faith of Jesus' resurrection and his other actions John called signs

Background

John 20

Main Idea

The signs Jesus did, supremely his resurrection, call us to faith in him as the Messiah.

Study and Action Emphases

- Share the gospel of Jesus Christ with all people
- Equip people for ministry in the church and in the world

Question to Explore

What leads a person to say, "I believe in Jesus," and mean it?

LESSON FOUR

So That You May Believe

Quick Read

For people who believe only when they see, Jesus' miracles and his resurrection offer the blessing of seeing because we believe. As Mary Magdalene and Thomas came to believe, so shall we when we encounter the risen Lord.

We sometimes say that seeing is believing. In God's way of doing things, though, believing is seeing. Even so, God does provide some help in leading us to believe even though we cannot see fully what is happening.

To this point, the Gospel of John has provided six signs to enable us to believe. (See "Signs in the Gospel of John.") There is one last sign to see. What if Jesus could die and rise again? Surely then everybody would believe.

When silent film star Rudolf Valentino died, historians say that 9,000 people passed by his casket every hour and the viewing lasted for three days! The Lord Jesus knew no such homage. Those who passed by his cross only taunted him. Only a few people came to his tomb— Nicodemus, Joseph of Arimathea, a few faithful women, and two apostles, Peter and John. But today thousands upon thousands have gone to Jerusalem to see the empty tomb even though it cannot be identified with certainty. Both the Garden Tomb and the Church of the Holy Sepulchre are *must* items on the agenda of every tourist. The homage paid to Rudolf Valentino, while considerable, did not last very long. The homage paid to the risen Christ has lasted for twenty centuries.

In John's account of the resurrection, we see real people. First we see Mary, who so desperately sought Christ after his death and saw first that he is alive. Second, we see the disciples to whom the resurrected Jesus appeared. Finally, we see Thomas, who had to see to believe.

Seeking to Believe (John 20:11–18)

Women were the last of Jesus' followers at the cross and the first at the tomb. Early on Sunday morning, Mary Magdalene discovered an empty tomb (20:1–2). Informing the disciples, she must have followed behind as Peter and John raced to the tomb and then left. But Mary could not leave.

Mary's persistent love for Jesus paid dividends. Mary looked again into the tomb. This time she saw angels there (20:12). As John 20:9 reminds us, the disciples, including Mary, did not understand about the resurrection. Mary was hoping against hope to see Christ again, wondering where his body had been taken.

A tombstone in a church cemetery in rural Louisiana marks a woman's grave under 150-year-old live oak trees. On her tombstone, in accord with her instructions, is the simple word, "Waiting!"

John 20:11–18, 26–31

[11] Mary stood outside the tomb crying. As she wept, she bent over to look into the tomb [12]and saw two angels in white, seated where Jesus' body had been, one at the head and the other at the foot.

[13]They asked her, "Woman, why are you crying?"

"They have taken my Lord away," she said, "and I don't know where they have put him." [14]At this, she turned around and saw Jesus standing there, but she did not realize that it was Jesus.

[15]"Woman," he said, "why are you crying? Who is it you are looking for?"

Thinking he was the gardener, she said, "Sir, if you have carried him away, tell me where you have put him, and I will get him."

[16]Jesus said to her, "Mary."

She turned toward him and cried out in Aramaic, "Rabboni!" (which means Teacher).

[17]Jesus said, "Do not hold on to me, for I have not yet returned to the Father. Go instead to my brothers and tell them, 'I am returning to my Father and your Father, to my God and your God.'"

[18]Mary Magdalene went to the disciples with the news: "I have seen the Lord!" And she told them that he had said these things to her.

· ·

[26]A week later his disciples were in the house again, and Thomas was with them. Though the doors were locked, Jesus came and stood among them and said, "Peace be with you!" [27]Then he said to Thomas, "Put your finger here; see my hands. Reach out your hand and put it into my side. Stop doubting and believe."

[28]Thomas said to him, "My Lord and my God!"

[29]Then Jesus told him, "Because you have seen me, you have believed; blessed are those who have not seen and yet have believed."

[30]Jesus did many other miraculous signs in the presence of his disciples, which are not recorded in this book. [31]But these are written that you may believe that Jesus is the Christ, the Son of God, and that by believing you may have life in his name.

Mary was waiting, and so are we. I have been to the graveside recently with the death of my grandmother. On a very cold day in Missouri, my parents, my brothers, and I walked to the corner of a cemetery where many in my family have been buried through the years. The only thing that sustained me on that cold day was the knowledge that because Jesus is risen, my grandmother was not there but with him.

The Gospel of John

If we envision reading the gospels as a stroll through a portrait gallery, we are immediately drawn to the Fourth Gospel. The Gospel of John represents for many the place where they first fell in love with Jesus. It is in John 3:16 that they first learned of God's great love. Believers and non-believers alike recognize the uniqueness of John's portrait of Jesus. Matthew, Mark, and Luke followed similar patterns in producing their individual stories of Christ, leading scholars to believe that all three are built on the same narrative. Matthew and Luke added to Mark's story their own special theological emphases.

In no way did John contradict the other three, but John's purpose was clearly different. While the other writers described numerous miracles Jesus performed, John built his gospel on seven specific *semeia* or signs. These signs consist of wonderful miracles performed for a purpose. They build in intensity from Jesus' seemingly reluctant miracle at Cana to a stunning, stirring crescendo in the resurrection. John recounted each successive story with the intention of eliciting faith. He wanted his readers to believe and experience the abundant eternal life of God.

Suddenly, Jesus was there with Mary. Incredibly, like the Jews of Jesus' day who had waited for a Messiah and missed him, Mary mistook her Lord for a gardener and asked where he had put Jesus' body. Perhaps Mary's grief had blinded her. One does not expect to see the deceased living again. Some suggest that Jesus' appearance had changed. Was Mary's vision obscured by the hazy morning light or by the abundance of her tears and depth of her sorrow? Whatever the case, when Mary heard the familiar intonation of Jesus' authoritative yet compassionate voice, recognition came. She ran to him.

Women were the last of Jesus' followers at the cross and the first at the tomb.

Jesus said, "'Do not hold on to me, for I have not yet returned to the Father. Go instead to my brothers and tell them, 'I am returning to my Father and your Father, to my God and your God'" (20:17). Are we surprised at Jesus' response? Why did he disallow her embrace? Some interpreters believe that Jesus' rebuke stems from the fact that his body was not yet the resurrected body. In other words, Jesus must still go to his Father, and so Mary could not hold on to his newly living body. Perhaps a better explanation rests in the practical understanding of the rest of the verse. The need for his disciples to know and believe took priority over the lasting embrace. In fact, Jesus rebuked her not for touching him as though he were untouchable, but rather for holding on when there were others who needed to know and believe. The conclusion of the verse demonstrates his great compassion as Jesus included Mary in a parent-child relationship to his Father. God was not only his Father but hers as well.

Isn't it interesting that Jesus chose not to reveal himself to Peter and John initially, but first to Mary? How shall we interpret the fact that a woman was the first to see the risen Lord? The story portends the teaching of Paul to the Galatians, "There is neither Jew nor Greek, slave nor free, male nor female, for you are all one in Christ Jesus" (Galatians 3:28). To all who would question the idea that God loves both genders inclusively, Mary's story provides a reminder that the power of Christ transcends gender distinctions and breaks down every barrier.

How shall we interpret the fact that a woman was the first to see the risen Lord?

Mary's love poured out in jubilant report to the disciples. She spoke not as one who had been rebuked, but as one who had been blessed. She exclaimed (20:18), "I have seen the Lord!" So he who had been her Lord in life had become Lord over death. Her obedience to him revealed her great love for him and faith in him.

Soon the other disciples would share her joy. On that very evening, Christ joined his disciples behind locked doors and offered them peace. Their joy knew no bounds as they saw the Lord. He offered them the Holy Spirit and conferred the power to forgive.

But not all of them were there. Thomas did not see, and so he did not believe.

Believing Is Seeing (20:26–31)

Don't be a doubting Thomas! That's what we sometimes say, isn't it? Thomas unwittingly gave us this expression. Forever and a day, Thomas will be associated with doubt. But John's story of Jesus tells a different story: Thomas is characterized first by resolute courage (11:16), second by reasonable curiosity (14:5), and ultimately by right conviction (20:28). Doubt was never a destination for Thomas; his doubt was just a roadside stop on the journey to strong faith.

Do you sometimes doubt? Do not despair. Your honest doubt may be the last stop before you arrive at the destination of conviction. Like

Thomas, you may just be on the way to coming to know Christ in a deeper way.

Thomas made the greatest confession of faith in John's Gospel when he exclaimed to Jesus (20:28), "My Lord and my God!" Because of Thomas, we get to hear perhaps the greatest beatitude of all (20:29): "'Blessed are those who have not seen and yet have believed!'" Of course, we would have loved to have been there and seen the empty tomb and the risen Christ. But we, like Thomases born out of time, have the privilege of believing without seeing. And if we avail ourselves of that opportunity, God promises us the joy of knowing Christ.

> Doubt was never a destination for Thomas; his doubt was just a roadside stop on the journey to strong faith.

Like Thomas, many of us won't believe because we cannot see (20:24–25). Thomas evidently came from the Ozark mountains of Galilee. He was a bonafide show-me-state Missourian, before there was a Missouri. Folks like this live in every state, of course. Thomas didn't see, and so he wouldn't believe. Before we are overly critical of Thomas, remember that the other disciples had seen Jesus before they believed. Only "the other disciple," whom I understand to be John, started to believe before he saw (20:8). Their faith was based upon what they had seen.

Thomas had made two mistakes. First, he had stayed away from the fellowship of faith (20:24). If we never fellowshipped with other believers,

Signs in the Gospel of John

One way that John distinguished his gospel was by referring to a select group of miracles he called *semeia* or signs. Each of these special miracles seeks to elicit a response of faith. Sometimes the people believe, and sometimes they do not. These miracles begin with the conversion of water to wine at Cana (2:1–11), move to the healing of the official's son (4:46–45), and continue with Jesus' healing the lame man at the pool of Bethesda (5:1–15), feeding the multitude (6:1–15), giving sight to the blind man (9:1–41), and raising Lazarus from the dead (11:1–44). They unveil to us a marvelous portrait of Jesus as the Son of God.

The story of the resurrection is the seventh or perfect sign. John explained the purpose of these signs by stating that there were many other signs, but these were "written that you may believe that Jesus is the Christ, the Son of God, and that by believing you may have life in his name" (20:31).

we would miss so much. We see in 20:19–23 that Jesus blessed the gathered disciples with peace and joy. Jesus breathed the Spirit into their lives and conferred authority on them to forgive sins. Thomas lived for eight days without the blessing Jesus wanted to give him. Whatever our bad experiences are, we must never allow them to isolate us from the community of faith. Had Thomas been with the community, he would have received earlier the blessing of seeing Jesus firsthand.

Your honest doubt may be the last stop before you arrive at the destination of conviction.

The second mistake Thomas made was that he demanded visible evidence. Thomas was apparently a highly rationalistic person, pessimistic and skeptical, who needed empirical proof. He believed that death was final. Notice in John 11:16 that he said, "Let us also go, that we may die with him." Thomas was honestly courageous. He was as ready to die with Jesus as any of the disciples were, but even in those words there is a sense of resignation as well as resolve. *If it is inevitable that we die, then let us die.* You hear it again in his words to the other ten (20:25): "Unless I see the nail marks in his hands and put my finger where the nails were, and put my hand into his side, I will not believe it." His final words are emphatic, as strong as the Greek allows—*I will never ever believe.* Thomas did not expect that Christ could be alive, and so he never intended to believe.

A story told about the astronomer Carl Sagan speaks of doubt and faith. Sagan was said to have been fascinated by the phenomenon that educated adults with the wonders of science all around them could cling to beliefs based on the unverifiable testimony of observers dead for 2000 years.

We never know until we believe.

The story goes that Sagan was talking with Joan Brown Campbell, a Christian leader, and said, "You're so smart, why do you believe in God?"

Joan Brown Campbell answered, "You're so smart, why don't you believe in God?"

The story continues that Sagan never wavered in his agnosticism. After Sagan's death, his wife said, "There was no deathbed conversion. No appeals to God, no hope for an afterlife, no pretending that they would see each other again." When asked whether Sagan wanted to believe, his wife fiercely replied, "Carl never wanted to believe. He wanted to know!"

How tragic! We never know until we believe.

Choosing Whom to Believe

An important substantiation of any religious group is whether what they teach actually happens. Remember the "Heaven's Gate" group that committed mass suicide in California and claimed that a UFO would take them away after they died? Of course, the UFO never showed. Jesus, on the other hand, predicted he would rise in three days, and he arose so that his disciples saw him. Jesus is risen.

So the claims of non-Christian groups cannot match the truth of Jesus' claims. Jesus claimed to be the resurrection and the life. He proved his claim by overthrowing death. One lesson we can take from this tragic story is this: If we choose to believe a Savior will raise us from death to life, we must be sure to choose one who has already done it.

An atheist approached a Quaker and asked, "Do you believe in God?"

The Quaker said, "Of course I do."

The atheist asked, "Well, have you ever seen God?"

The Quaker responded, "Well, no."

The atheist asked, "Have you ever touched God?"

The Quaker answered, "No."

The atheist continued, "Have you ever felt God?"

The Quaker replied, "No."

Jesus still comes to all of us and to each of us.

The atheist asked, "What makes you think there is a God?"

The Quaker looked at the atheist and said, "Let me ask thee a question. Hast thou ever seen thy brain?"

The atheist answered, "No."

The Quaker asked, "Hast thou ever felt thy brain?"

The atheist answered, "No."

The Quaker asked, "Hast thou ever touched thy brain?"

The atheist answered, "No."

The Quaker concluded by asking, "What makes thee think thou hast a brain?"

Thomas had seen Jesus die, and so he knew Jesus was dead. That is why he couldn't believe. Many modern skeptics attempt to justify their unbelief by suggesting that the disciples just wanted to believe so badly that they invented the resurrection as a symbol of life. However, to tell a dying man that the resurrection is only a symbol of new life is like giving a starving man a picture of food and telling him to be full!

We cannot help but notice the way Jesus came to his disciples as a group and then came to Thomas personally and individually. Jesus still comes to all of us and to each of us.

We cannot see Jesus with our eyes. But we can believe in him!

When Jesus came to Thomas personally, Thomas realized that Jesus heard every word he had spoken and still came to him. Isn't this a pattern with God? When Adam and Eve sinned, God went looking for them. When the world was lost in sin, God came personally. When Jesus' disciples were afraid, he came to them. And when one disciple missed the opportunity, Jesus came back just for him. I would have been tempted to say, as a professor might, "Get the notes and study them yourself. I'm not going to this extra trouble."

When Jesus came personally to Thomas and gave him peace, Thomas didn't need to touch Jesus' hands and side. Thomas believed and exclaimed (20:28), "My Lord and my God!"

On a trip to the Holy Land, we saw a number of tombs. We saw David's tomb, Absalom's tomb, and the tombs of Haggai, Malachi, and Zechariah. We also saw the tomb in the garden near Gordon's Calvary. The difference in the tombs was overwhelming to me. Our tour guide said there were still bones in all the tombs except in that simple tomb in the

What if doubt is an opportunity for faith?

garden. Whoever had been buried there was gone. I watched as people walked in and wept. Then I took my turn. And there in the tomb, I stayed and stared for the longest time. He was not there. He had risen. He is alive! But you don't have to see that tomb to believe. I believed before I ever entered the tomb. The proof is a risen Savior: Jesus is alive.

Mary Magdalene believed when she saw Jesus; so did the other ten disciples. But Thomas had the chance to believe without seeing. And we have that same chance today. We cannot see Jesus with our eyes. But we can believe in him! Will we believe in him? I challenge you to read the story of Jesus in the Gospel of John and still not believe. If we are honestly seeking him, Jesus promises we will find him!

Like Thomas we can lament our lost opportunities. But what if our disadvantages are advantages? What if doubt is an opportunity for faith?

QUESTIONS

1. Look at the signs Jesus performed in the Gospel of John (2:1–11; 4:46–54; 5:1–15; 6:1–15; 9:1–41; 11:1–44; 20:1–31). What do you notice about the progression? Do the signs lead you to believe? How has that belief changed your life?

2. Mary grieved in the garden alone. Thomas struggled with his doubts by himself. How has the community of a church family helped you to work through your grief and doubts? Do you have grief or doubts that you can share with your Bible study group?

3. Which of the explanations of Jesus' response to Mary in John 20:17 do you like best? Why?

4. Compare Thomas' confession of Jesus' identity in 20:28 to previous confessions of disciples in John's Gospel (see 4:29; 5:11; 9:35–38).

5. How does John's conclusion in 20:30–31 inform readers about the purpose of this gospel? In what ways does the portrait of Jesus in John's Gospel inform your understanding of who Jesus is? How does John's Gospel enrich your faith?

The Ministry of Jesus Continues

The Acts of the Apostles is aptly named. The book portrays the acts of the early disciples and apostles as they lived their faith. On the surface, this piece of literature may strike the reader as only history. More accurately, it should be called sacred history. Luke continued the narrative begun in his gospel. The reader can ascertain a distinct sense from Luke of "here is where Christianity went." We are indebted to Luke for putting into words some of the things that happened with the beginning of Christianity.

This unit of three lessons will inform the reader regarding these early accounts of where the apostles went and what they did. Luke intended to demonstrate how Jesus continued his ministry in the actions of the early church. Each generation can sense Luke's challenge, however. That is, we must consider how Jesus yet continues his ministry in our lives and churches.

Lesson five notes the connection between Jesus' ministry as it began, Jesus' promise of the Holy Spirit for the disciples, and the expected extension of witness. The disciples would be empowered to witness in ways they had not thought possible before. Both lesson six and lesson seven demonstrate who can be saved and how salvation happens. Lesson six considers, as well, the telling and preaching of the gospel. Lesson seven reviews the challenge of the gospel's inclusiveness, particularly as the Jerusalem Council grappled with this issue. At this council, the church affirmed that salvation is by grace through faith.[1]

UNIT TWO: THE MINISTRY OF JESUS CONTINUES

NOTES

1. Unless otherwise indicated, all Scripture quotes in Unit 2, Lessons 5–7, are from the New Revised Standard Version.

Focal Text
Acts 1:1–9; 2:43–47

Background
Acts 1—2

Main Idea
As we are empowered by the Holy Spirit to witness about Jesus in our words and deeds, we share in his continued ministry.

Question to Explore
How does Jesus' ministry continue today?

Study Aim
To decide to yield to the Holy Spirit's power and witness about Jesus in my words and deeds

Study and Action Emphases
- Share the gospel of Jesus Christ with all people
- Minister to human needs in the name of Jesus Christ
- Equip people for ministry in the church and in the world
- Develop Christian families
- Strengthen existing churches and start new congregations

LESSON FIVE

Sharing in Jesus' Continued Ministry

Quick Read
Too many Christians live today as if Jesus never came out of the tomb. But Jesus rose again, visited with his disciples, and left a charge to keep going on the job. Once we wrap our minds and hearts around that idea, we can truly say, *That is the best news I have ever heard.*

Several years ago, I sat with one of the more famous theologians of our time. He related an experience in which someone had asked why he did not leave the Christian faith. That person pressed the point and added, "Why don't you join the movement of blending the major religious faiths?"

The theologian replied, "I cannot do that. We Christians consider Jesus Christ and what he stands for to be a unique happening. We have been saying that for two thousand years. I will continue to state and act upon that idea."

Acts 1:1–9

[1]In the first book, Theophilus, I wrote about all that Jesus did and taught from the beginning [2]until the day when he was taken up to heaven, after giving instructions through the Holy Spirit to the apostles whom he had chosen. [3]After his suffering he presented himself alive to them by many convincing proofs, appearing to them during forty days and speaking about the kingdom of God. [4]While staying with them, he ordered them not to leave Jerusalem, but to wait there for the promise of the Father. "This," he said, "is what you have heard from me; [5]for John baptized with water, but you will be baptized with the Holy Spirit not many days from now."

[6]So when they had come together, they asked him, "Lord, is this the time when you will restore the kingdom to Israel?" [7]He replied, "It is not for you to know the times or periods that the Father has set by his own authority. [8]But you will receive power when the Holy Spirit has come upon you; and you will be my witnesses in Jerusalem, in all Judea and Samaria, and to the ends of the earth." [9]When he had said this, as they were watching, he was lifted up, and a cloud took him out of their sight.

Acts 2:43–47

[43]Awe came upon everyone, because many wonders and signs were being done by the apostles. [44]All who believed were together and had all things in common; [45]they would sell their possessions and goods and distribute the proceeds to all, as any had need. [46]Day by day, as they spent much time together in the temple, they broke bread at home and ate their food with glad and generous hearts, [47]praising God and having the goodwill of all the people. And day by day the Lord added to their number those who were being saved.

Indeed, what Jesus demonstrated through his mission and ministry did not end with his death or even his ascension. The impetus continues into the very day you read these words.

Empowerment for Continuing (Acts 1:1–11)

When we read Acts 1:1 from the New Revised Standard Version, we get the impression that Jesus did and taught—in the past tense. The New International Version (NIV) and the New American Standard Bible (NASB) communicate the meaning in a way that is more accurate to the Greek text, however. Luke's meaning refers to "all that Jesus *began* to do and to teach" (NIV, NASB; italics for emphasis). Rather than something stopping, perhaps in midstream, the action started and continues to the reader's own time.

Luke recounted Jesus' final days with the disciples. In a quick review, Luke let his readers know of Jesus' death (suffering) and resurrection. These are basic premises of the gospel.

One of the few references we have of Jesus' appearances for forty days after his resurrection comes here. We can only employ our "holy imaginations" to consider what Jesus may have done and said during those days as he gave "many convincing proofs" and as he spoke "about the kingdom of God" (1:3).

The Book of Acts

If we had only the Gospel of Matthew, Mark, Luke, or John—or even all four of them—we might ask, "What else happened?" The Book of Acts answers that question.

The Book of Acts is the second volume of Luke's account of the beginnings of the Christian movement. In the first volume, Luke described "all that Jesus began to do and to teach" (Acts 1:1, NIV). Now, in this second volume, which we call the Book of Acts, Luke continued the story of what Jesus *continued* to do and to teach in the life of the early church.

Like a good sequel writer, Luke reviewed just enough of the major thrust of his Gospel to remind his audience where the story had been. We are not sure whether Theophilus was a literal person (1:1). The word "Theophilus" literally means *lover of God.* One possibility is that Luke used a term that could mean "God lover" as a way of introducing the account to any reader.

Note in 1:4 that Jesus commanded the disciples to remain in Jerusalem. Think of the kinds of pressures the disciples must have felt to leave, even escape, Jerusalem after the events of Jesus'crucifixion and resurrection.

Jesus instructed the disciples, however, to wait before they acted. An image that comes to mind is that of charging a battery. There is a point at which the battery will dispense its energy; however, it must get charged first.

Waiting is important for our own "acts of Christian disciples." Waiting helps us avoid acting too quickly, without considering the consequences. We sometimes attempt acts of witness and ministry before a time of spiritual formation.

> Jesus calls us to be patient and wait to receive his power also.

We can be active in doing things but lack the depth and maturity for the task. The charge to proclaim the gospel to the world is daunting. All of us at one time or another realize we are too weak and fainthearted for what we are called upon to do. We need the undergirding of Christ's Spirit.

Jesus so much as said to the disciples gathered around him, *Be patient. The time is coming when I will be going. The Spirit is coming. The will, the courage, and the energy for the work will come, too.* Jesus calls us to be patient and wait to receive his power also.

Pentecost

Pentecost literally means "fifty days." Pentecost was part of a festival observed by the Jews. This festival commemorated God's great acts in Jewish history. The first annual festival on the fourteenth day of the first month of the Jewish calendar was Passover. This month would coincide generally with our March-April. Recall that Jesus was crucified during Passover.

The second major annual Jewish festival was Pentecost, which came seven weeks or fifty days after Passover. During this festival, Jews celebrated the first fruits of the harvest. Loaves of bread were baked from the first harvested grain. Thus, the Feast of Weeks, the Feast of Harvest, or the Day of First fruits (all names used to designate the festival) commenced.

The background for Pentecost can be reviewed from passages such as Exodus 23:16; 34:22; Numbers 28:26; Leviticus 23:15–16; and Deuteronomy 16:10.

The coming of the Holy Spirit corresponded to the coming of the first fruits. The first fruits symbolized the promise of the complete harvest that was to come (see Romans 8:23).

Does this question the disciples asked in 1:6 strike you as being odd: "Lord, is this the time when you will restore the kingdom to Israel?" After all the time Jesus had taken to go over with the disciples the what, why, and even the how of his mission and ministry, Jesus had to continue educating them. They continued to hold presuppositions that the kingdom would be political in nature. Perhaps only because we have the benefit of hindsight, we realize how they missed the point.

> *As Peter wove Old Testament texts into his sermon, he demonstrated that Jesus' incarnation fit into a seamless flow of revelation from God.*

Interestingly, Jesus merely deflected this question and moved to the heart of the issue. The waiting was coming to an end for the disciples. A transition was about to occur.

Acts 1:8 has been called the summation of Acts, an outline of the book in one verse. The disciples had seen the miracles of Jesus, had witnessed the resurrection, and had participated in post-resurrection conversation with Jesus. Still, however, they lacked a reference point for much of what was yet to be. Look carefully at Jesus' statement, "You will receive power when the Holy Spirit has come upon you" (1:8).

Empowerment is a word used often in some circles these days. Sometimes it seems to be just a "buzz word" and thus faddish and empty. The idea in 1:8 fills to overflowing the concept, though. The "power" of the Holy Spirit would carry energy. The Greek term for "power" in this verse is one from which we draw our English word *dynamite*. Imagine the power! The same word gives rise to our term *dynamic*. Imagine the vitality—power for energy, power for obtaining a goal, and power left over!

Further, still in verse 8, Jesus outlined the task to be fulfilled and where to do it. The disciples were to tell what they had seen and experienced with Jesus. Furthermore, they were not to let geographical boundaries or ethnic boundaries hinder their sharing the gospel. A three-layered approach was to be utilized: witness in Jerusalem (where you are); witness in Judea and Samaria (your region); witness to the ends of the earth (the whole world).

As if punctuating this point, Jesus ascended from the disciples' sight (1:9). The disciples stood, "gazing" (1:10)—likely as we would, too. Two heavenly messengers chided these disciples for their preoccupation with this event. Of course, the disciples had just beheld a monumental happening.

Fellowship

Consider these ideas for increasing the level of Christian fellowship in and beyond your congregation.

1. Study the term *koinonia* (or fellowship) through finding in a concordance places in which the word is used, discovering the definition of the word in a Bible dictionary, and/or doing additional study of Acts 2:43–47 in a commentary. Outline the points of what constituted *koinonia* for the early Christians—for example, worship together, meals together, financial support.

2. Develop a "supper club" with interested members. Form groups of four to eight members who will schedule a once-a-month time to eat out together or have a potluck dinner. Encourage the groups to include those who are not part of your Sunday School or church membership.

Still, we might understand the messengers' remarks to the disciples like this (1:11): *Your question of Jesus' coming back is basically answered. It will be much like what you have just seen. There is much work to be done, however. So, be about it, now!* And, that is our charge, as well.

The Spirit Comes (1:12—2:42)

We can understand by implication that the ascension happened on Mount Olivet, not far from Jerusalem. We might expect the disciples to do something next that was earthshaking. They entered, though, into the process of choosing a successor to Judas Iscariot's position. Perhaps they had not done this before simply because they were in the Lord's presence and had more important things about which to think.

A sign of some changing dynamics arose as Peter announced that a new apostle must be selected. As recorded in 1:20, Peter took his rationale from Psalms 69:25; 109:8. Nominations were made, a vote was taken, and Mathias was elected. The disciples, only about 120 people, continued meeting together, likely for fellowship and security (Acts 1:15). They were together as the Jewish festival of Pentecost commenced.

What happened in this gathering is described vividly in 2:1–12. Note that Luke related that the sound was "like the rush of a violent wind" and the sight was "divided tongues, as of fire" (2:2–3). Although Luke did his best to describe the sight, he yet found the phenomenon to be almost indescribable. He described what happened as "like" events with which his readers might have been familiar. Many present then, and many who first read Luke's words, would have understood what these representations depicted. The wind and fire were methods by which God had revealed himself in the Old Testament era.

Their relationships to one another were affected so deeply that anytime anyone needed anything, property would be sold, and a common pot of money would be used to meet the needs.

The new phenomenon was the speaking and hearing of languages—the miracle of communication. This action drew the response of being "amazed and astonished" from those who experienced the event (2:7). Luke further described the situation with the words "amazed and perplexed" (2:12). The addition of the idea of being perplexed shows the crowd's divided opinion. Some asked (2:12), "'What does this mean?'" Others merely sneered.

Peter again addressed the crowd in one of the most fully recorded sermons in the New Testament (2:14–36). This sermon is an extraordinary example of how one can defend and explain the Christian faith and also offer it for others to receive. Note that Peter had moved from a rather cowardly approach about his faith, as when he had denied Jesus three times, to one of forthrightness and courage.

Peter made a connection to the Book of Joel in the Old Testament, likely for the benefit of the primarily Jewish audience (see especially Joel 2:28–29). Peter was able to show in the context of the Jews' history that this appearance of the Spirit among them was wholly in keeping with how God acted and what God had promised. In addition, Peter succinctly yet profoundly related the content of the gospel. He drew attention to Jesus' ministry

With worship being a priority, all other relationships fell into proper place.

and miracles (Acts 2:22) and to Jesus' crucifixion and resurrection (2:23–24).

As Peter wove Old Testament texts into his sermon, he demonstrated that Jesus' incarnation fit into a seamless flow of revelation from God. Rather than being surprised by all that had happened, the audience should have been expecting these kinds of events.

Luke described the audience's response to Peter's sermon with the words, "cut to the heart" (2:37), meaning *laid bare*. The people realized their distance from God, especially in how they had treated Jesus. They asked (2:37), "'What should we do?'" Peter responded, "Repent" (2:38). He was saying that the people should turn from their sin and turn their lives over to God.

Peter continued pressing the point with comments Luke did not record (2:40). Peter became an instrument for the working of the Spirit in many people's lives. "About three thousand" were saved and baptized (2:41).

In Acts 2:42, notice that the new believers demonstrated that the Christian life is not just about being a spectator of supernatural events. The new believers' newfound faith prodded them toward a relationship of genuine fellowship with one another.

Life Together (2:43–47)

One of the prominent theologians of the twentieth century, Dietrich Bonhoeffer, wrote a book about congregational life called *Life Together*. Where the reader might expect ideas stated so abstractly as not to be understandable, he or she will find a simple, but not simplistic, presentation of ideas very close to what is portrayed in Acts 2:43–47.

Note first that the people responded with awe because of the "wonders and signs" being "done by the apostles" (2:43). "Awe" is an excellent word for worship. Reverence marked these early Christians' approach to life. They realized that one's relationship to God through Jesus Christ was more important than anything else. With worship being a priority, all other relationships fell into proper place.

> *Meeting together for a meal can still be a good way to meet new people and deepen relationships with old friends.*

We can well imagine that wherever the apostles went, whomever they saw, they performed signs and miracles as the Lord Jesus had done when he was present physically. They were continuing Jesus' ministry, empowered by the Spirit. The miracles were not to draw attention to the apostles. Indeed, as Jesus had done, the apostles were demonstrating the presence of the kingdom of God.

Notice also in 2:44 how Luke commented about the disciples' relationships with each other regarding material goods. The matters about which people are usually the most secretive and protective in our society—material goods—were those that the Christians in Jerusalem held in common. Only a little is said about the administrative side of this system, how it worked. What we see clearly, however, is that the early Christians found their common relationship to Jesus as Lord of life to be paramount to anything else. Their relationships to one another were affected so deeply that anytime anyone needed anything, property would be sold, and a common pot of money would be used to meet the needs.

If our churches practiced koinonia *more faithfully, would we have so many divisions, so many internal conflicts, and so many breakdowns in relationships?*

Moreover, the people enjoyed being with one another. They worshiped together.

Furthermore, those early Christians met together at mealtime and in one another's homes. Undoubtedly the food varied in both quality and quantity. However, these Christians ate together with "glad and generous hearts" (2:46). Meeting together for a meal can still be a good way to meet new people and deepen relationships with old friends. In our time, this is one facet of what can be called hospitality evangelism. Gathering around a meal in someone's home can be an effective way today to enable people not familiar with faith in Christ to see Christian people "up close and personal." In such a context, conversation about faith can be quite natural.

Truly the people in Acts enjoyed one another. They operated out of a common bond through the Lordship of Christ.

Contemporary readers may dismiss the church's activities in Acts 2:43–47 too quickly. Comments follow such lines as this: *Oh, this was a very special time in the life of the church. It had to happen this way in order for the gospel to make an immediate impact.* Or, we may hear this thought: *The modern world is just too complex for such a simple arrangement to work now.* Yet another perspective limits "fellowship" to get-togethers at a church building or someone's house.

We do well to look more closely, however, at what was happening in the life of the early church in this passage and see how it applies to us. Too many churches fail to understand and apply the principles of *koinonia* (the Greek word for fellowship) that the early church demonstrated. If our churches practiced *koinonia* more faithfully, would we have so many divisions, so many internal conflicts, and so many breakdowns in relationships? Would we not care for fellow believers more deeply?

The Jerusalem Christians present a lovely picture of what "life together" should be like for Christians. Many contemporary Christians experience something of what they did. I know Christians whose relationships to their fellow church folk are wonderful. They have a closer relationship to some in the family of Christian faith than with some of their own blood-kin. These kinds of relationships portray to one another and to the world at large what it means to share in Jesus' continued ministry.

QUESTIONS

1. Jesus lives, moves among us, and gives us purpose in life—right now! How would you relate that thought to people you know?

2. How have you experienced the power of the Holy Spirit?

3. Why do many contemporary Christians not relate to one another as the early church did in Acts 2:43–47?

4. Consider the dimensions of your local church's life together. What are the positive points? What suggestions do you have about how relationships in your local church could improve?

Focal Text
Acts 10:34–48

Background
Acts 10

Main Idea
We are to share the gospel of Jesus with everyone, inviting them to accept him by faith.

Question to Explore
What is the gospel, and who is it for?

Study Aim
To develop a caring approach to sharing the gospel

Study Emphases and Actions
- Share the gospel of Jesus Christ with all people
- Equip people for ministry in the church and in the world

LESSON SIX

Telling the Story of Jesus

Quick Read
The gospel is intended to be open and offered to anyone and everyone. Too often, Christians decide on the basis of their prejudices as to whom the story of Jesus will be told.

In the last chapel address that T. B. Maston made at Southwestern Seminary, he spoke about "The Unfinished Agenda." In that address, Maston noted that particularly with regard to race relations, Baptists had made some progress but not enough. He made these comments in light of Scripture passages like the one in this lesson. For Maston, Christians let culturally shaped views have more control over how and to whom they relate than they do the story and the actions of the gospel.

Acts 10:34–48

34Then Peter began to speak to them: "I truly understand that God shows no partiality, 35but in every nation anyone who fears him and does what is right is acceptable to him. 36You know the message he sent to the people of Israel, preaching peace by Jesus Christ—he is Lord of all. 37That message spread throughout Judea, beginning in Galilee after the baptism that John announced: 38how God anointed Jesus of Nazareth with the Holy Spirit and with power; how he went about doing good and healing all who were oppressed by the devil, for God was with him. 39We are witnesses to all that he did both in Judea and in Jerusalem. They put him to death by hanging him on a tree; 40but God raised him on the third day and allowed him to appear, 41not to all the people but to us who were chosen by God as witnesses, and who ate and drank with him after he rose from the dead. 42He commanded us to preach to the people and to testify that he is the one ordained by God as judge of the living and the dead. 43All the prophets testify about him that everyone who believes in him receives forgiveness of sins through his name."

44While Peter was still speaking, the Holy Spirit fell upon all who heard the word. 45The circumcised believers who had come with Peter were astounded that the gift of the Holy Spirit had been poured out even on the Gentiles, 46for they heard them speaking in tongues and extolling God. Then Peter said, 47"Can anyone withhold the water for baptizing these people who have received the Holy Spirit just as we have?" 48So he ordered them to be baptized in the name of Jesus Christ. Then they invited him to stay for several days.

Clean? Unclean? (10:1–16)

The terms *clean* and *unclean* are not used typically in our circles. The Jews of the New Testament era considered them regularly, however. The origin of the concepts behind these terms can be read in Leviticus 11:1–47 and

Deuteronomy 14:1–21. The instructions in these chapters communicated to the ancient Hebrews that certain animals and kinds of animals were not to be eaten.

The matter of uncleanness, in addition, transferred to individuals who ate, or even touched the carcass of, an animal on the unclean list. Because these guidelines were part of the larger pattern of worship, the logic was simple in connecting an unclean animal to a person, thus considering that person to be unclean and thus unholy.

Jews divided society into clean and unclean people—those who adhered closely to the ritual laws of Judaism and those who did not. The emphasis came to be placed on external, ritual cleanness rather than on internal, moral cleanness.

These thoughts can help the reader understand the context as Jesus related to the ritual law. The scribes and Pharisees put a high premium on detailed attention to rituals. Jesus reissued God's call to moral cleanness rather than ritual cleanness.

As well, the Jews had turned the ideas of clean and unclean so as to amplify prejudices that inevitably enter the conversation when people are divided into groups. For the Jews, one who exhibited a ritually unclean life was inferior. One was not to touch or engage in conversation with such a person.

The distance between the use of *clean* and *unclean* during Peter's time and ours is not so far, actually. Of course, we generally do not divide people according to what we eat or do not eat. Certainly, however, we have other ways we divide society. The division may be according to skin color, language, ethnic/cultural background, or economic level.

The basis for these kinds of divisions usually reflects a kind of prejudicial treatment of others. Prejudice means "prejudging" another, based on incomplete information.

Misinformation and prejudging on incomplete information—such become the basis for judging people as clean and unclean. Such erroneous notions and practices are the context for the narrative in Acts 10. Luke presented in a vivid way how God intended clean and unclean to be understood. The larger context teaches about how one comes to faith in Christ and how one who is a Christian should relate the gospel.

At the least, Luke's account is an excellent example of how to relate a story. The reader's interest is caught immediately with the introduction of a man who held a prominent position in his community.

Cornelius was posted at Caesarea, a city established by Herod the Great in honor of Augustus Caesar. As a Roman soldier, Cornelius was a centurion, one who commanded a body of one hundred men. His group was part of a larger group known as a cohort. A cohort was about six hundred men or one tenth of a legion.

Experience with God demonstrates that more insight comes as we need more clarity.

Cornelius was not a Jew by birth. He practiced Judaism to the extent he could, however. As a non-Jew, he could not be involved in temple sacrifices. Still, Cornelius used the time ordinarily given to sacrifice to pray. Luke left no doubt that Cornelius was a man of circumspect character.

The other major character, Peter, was down the coast from Caesarea at Joppa. Furthermore, he was staying with another Simon, a tanner. This man was likely a Christian. A Jew would not have been involved in this trade since animals declared unclean in the Torah would have been used in the tanning of hides.

The extraordinary process by which Peter came to understand the real meaning of the terms *clean* and *unclean* demonstrates how deeply some prejudices are ingrained in us. As well, we can realize that the depth of these prejudices requires a spiritual turnaround on our part if we are to deal with these prejudices in a Christlike manner.

Acting Out of Understanding (Acts 10:17–33)

Acts 10:17–33 provides models for what we are to do with the information God gives us. Cornelius and Peter demonstrate two perspectives. Cornelius hears, initiates further inquiry, and acts on further information. Peter hears, does not understand immediately, but gradually acts more forcefully and passionately on what he understands.

Note that Cornelius heard and understood his vision the first time (Acts 10:1–6). Note, too, that Cornelius followed the instructions from his vision and had messengers on their way to Joppa even before Peter had his vision. On the other hand, Peter had to have his vision conveyed three times. Before we castigate Peter, let us recall those times when our spiritual insight came slowly.

An essential purpose of Luke's narrative was to convey the movement of God in the lives of people. Note in this passage how God brought

Centurion

Centurions formed the backbone of the Roman army. Indeed, many times they were the backbone of the Roman Empire. The title *centurion* finds its basis in "century" or one hundred. Each centurion commanded one hundred men.

By virtue of their positions, centurions could be people of some financial means. Perhaps a usual perception is that these centurions were only rough, raw personalities. Cornelius was perceived as a man of honor by the Jews, however. He was headquartered in Caesarea to serve with the procurator of Judea, Samaria, and Idumea.

A centurion appears more often on the pages of the New Testament than we may realize. In fact, a centurion often is present at key points in the events of the New Testament. See passages such as Matthew 8:5–13; 27:45–56; Acts 10:1–48; 21:27–40; 22:22–29; 23:12–35; 24:10–23; 27:1–44.

---

together two men, some distance apart, through separate visions. Perhaps we do well also to reflect on why God was able to communicate to Cornelius and Peter through visions. Were the daily, conscious lives of Cornelius and Peter so full that God had to communicate through a more subconscious mode? What does this mean for how God communicates to us?

The passage provides an example of the best style of relationships for religious people to demonstrate.

Peter was still puzzled by his vision, as we likely would be, even as Cornelius' emissaries arrived. God's Spirit may have been giving information to Peter at the pace Peter could best comprehend. All of us can relate times when spiritual insight came rather quickly and other times when we were quite slow getting the point. Peter teaches us that we need to move with the light and understanding we have. Experience with God demonstrates that more insight comes as we need more clarity.

Two visions that occurred more than thirty miles apart began to come together in the conversation between Peter and Cornelius' messengers. We have no details of the conversation besides the basic reason these men came from Joppa. Note that in addition to Peter and the three messengers, other Christian believers, perhaps including Simon the tanner, may have been involved in the conversation.

One way our imaginations could carry us is to think of this group sitting up late into the night. Picture Peter relating his vision. Imagine that next the three from Joppa related what they knew about Cornelius.

Perhaps Peter spoke of the day of Pentecost, of his experiences of walking with Jesus himself, of his upbringing as a Jew, of how his understanding of what it means to be a Christian had taken shape. That would have been a marvelous, delightful conversation in which to have taken part.

Luke related the journey to Joppa as being a day and a half. The implication is that the messengers from Caesarea and the group traveling up from Joppa walked the trip. One option was to have gone by boat, since both cities were seacoast cities. However the groups traveled, each made the trip rather quickly. Likely both parties felt invigorated by the subject at hand. God was moving in their midst. The people involved became enthusiastic about discovering what would come next.

A watershed event happened in this encounter of Cornelius and Peter.

Note that not only Peter but also other believers from Joppa accompanied him. Think about what these people talked about as they made their way up to Caesarea. Consider the importance that was placed on this trip in that several people evidently dropped their day-to-day activities to go with Peter.

Luke does not convey how Cornelius had such certainty that anyone would come from Joppa. Preparations were made for a party of travelers, though. The implication is that God was moving.

Cornelius knew about how long the trip would take for someone to come up from Joppa. Remember he was a centurion and likely had made the march to and from Joppa many times. He invited relatives and close friends to be there, ready to meet the group coming.

The call to salvation addresses every aspect of our lives, including our work.

The image of Cornelius falling at Peter's feet is striking (10:25). A further striking feature is Peter's response of humility (10:26). This comment and action alone is a worthy lesson to draw from this passage. The passage provides an example of the best style of relationships for religious people to demonstrate. Too many religious leaders take a position of prestige and power toward others. Too often, the consequences are that such an attitude of superiority gets in the way of communicating the gospel.

The next part of the exchange between Cornelius and Peter indicates the profound change in Peter's thinking. Peter did not go into as much detail about his vision as Cornelius did regarding his own. Yet, Peter's words clearly indicate he was convinced the gospel was not only for Jews but for Gentiles as well.

A watershed event happened in this encounter of Cornelius and Peter. Luke considered the account so important that Acts 11 recounts the happening as Peter reported to the church at Jerusalem. With the gospel extended to Cornelius and his household, the early church began turning to the Gentile world.

What Is the Story of Jesus? (Acts 10:34–48)

Remember that Luke was relating what we might call the first history of the early church. Thus Luke indeed related the *acts* of the apostles. Even more important, Luke related the *acts* of the Holy Spirit among people.

The accounts are fascinating. Rather than holding the facts at an objective, impersonal distance, however, we are called to participate

Are we willing for God to address our own prejudice?

in them. Luke put forward examples that call us to consider the cultural context in which we live and how we are responding to it. Furthermore, Luke provided some fairly simple outlines of what the story of Jesus is and how to communicate that story.

Peter had a captivated audience even before he began his sermon that begins in 10:34. Cornelius swung wide open the door to his soul and the souls of those assembled at his house. God had prepared them for receiving what Peter had to say.

Often we mistakenly think we are the ones doing the hard work of spreading the gospel. Actually, God moves ahead of us, preparing this one and that one to hear what we have to say. What are we to do? We are to be ready to give a word about Jesus.

Peter began by telling that he had learned that God was impartial toward people who respond to him. Peter now knew that God does not go by human standards of race and ethnic background to determine whether God will accept people (10:35).

Peter's sermon was short and simple—not a bad model in itself. In many ways the sermon is similar to other sermons in Acts. The basic outline of the early church's preaching of the gospel is here.

Peter began by referring to Cornelius' previous knowledge of the gospel message (10:36). Observe that Peter drew attention in 10:36 to Jesus'

Evangelism: People Coming to Us

Too many Christians carry the image of evangelism as being only that of going to others. We may not recognize often enough the need to respond to inquirers such as Cornelius. Here are some questions to consider to help you recognize and act on this truth:

- How well do your church's worship services and programming communicate the essentials of the gospel to "outsiders" who come to inquire about the Christian faith?
- Does your Sunday School class have ways to respond to inquirers about Christian faith?
- List ways you could respond to someone who said to you, "So now all of us are here in the presence of God to listen to all that the Lord has commanded you to say" (Acts 10:33).

message of peace as Peter spoke with Cornelius, a man trained in war. The call to salvation addresses every aspect of our lives, including our work.

In 10:37–38, Peter recalled from his own experience of Jesus' mission and ministry the places Jesus went and the miracles Jesus did. Sometimes Christians do not consider these points important to relate to non-believers. Rather, we jump quickly to the death, burial, and resurrection of Jesus. Do not forget, however, that much of the content of the gospels is given to Jesus' life and ministry as he proclaimed the kingdom.

In 10:39–43, Peter related Jesus' crucifixion, resurrection, post-resurrection appearances, and commission. This commission is to go and tell the message and thus call others to experience forgiveness.

The Holy Spirit moved upon those present. This event has been called the Gentile Pentecost. Similar to what happened in Jerusalem among only Jews, or former Jews, this event made the point that the gospel was to move among those before declared unclean.

Peter's next comment (10:47) further indicates where the larger group of early Christians would move with regard to inclusion in their fellowship. Peter asked whether anyone could refuse baptism to these people. If those with Peter rebuked his question, they would have to declare their own experiences of faith and fellowship to be invalid.

Note in 10:48 the place of baptism and its relation to salvation. Note also that Peter evidently did not baptize any at this gathering at Cornelius' house. Rather, Peter instructed those with him to do this act.

Cornelius and his friends asked Peter to stay several more days. Did the other Christians from Joppa stay, too? We do not know. How long is "several"? We do not know. What did Peter and Cornelius talk about? My guess is that Cornelius asked for more details from Peter. Cornelius probably asked questions such as these: What was it like to have actually worked with Jesus? What is it like to have done miracles yourself? How are you doing after your denial of Jesus? How can I be a powerful witness like you are?

We have no further information about Cornelius in the New Testament. My guess, however, is that Cornelius became a stirring witness to the story of Jesus.

Maybe this study of Acts 10 not only has inspired you but also encouraged you toward telling the story of Jesus. Still, the events Luke related for us seem almost too simple. A man's heart was stirred by God. The man sent for help to address this stirring. God

Are we willing to let God send us out to share the gospel with all people?

convinced a prejudiced believer to overcome his prejudice and go and tell the gospel story. The believer did just that. A group assembled and heard the gospel gladly, welcoming Jesus as Lord of their lives. The group then enjoyed Christian fellowship with one another, unhindered by the prejudice of their culture.

We know that sometimes we find it difficult to reach out to all people with the gospel. We also may find it especially difficult to enter into genuine fellowship with people who are different from us in some ways, even though they are Christians.

Thus, this lesson calls us to ask ourselves some important questions. Are we willing for God to address our own prejudice? Are we willing to let God send us out to share the gospel with all people? The story of the salvation of Cornelius and his household puts the burden of proof on us as to whether we are willing to respond to God's call to share the gospel with all people.

QUESTIONS

1. Reflect on how God communicated to Cornelius and Peter through visions. Would you consider this a viable way for God to communicate to us today?

2. Consider times in which you have sensed the impression from God to share the gospel with others. How did you react? Did you relate this experience to other Christians? How was your intent to be a witness to the gospel strengthened by this mutual sharing of witnessing experiences?

3. Outline the points of the gospel story in Acts 10:36–43. Which points have been most meaningful to you in your experiences? How do these experiences both validate and clarify how you tell the story of Jesus to others?

Focal Text

Acts 15:1–21

Background

Acts 11:19–26;
13:44–52;
14:24—15:35

Main Idea

God graciously offers
salvation to all people
on the basis of their
faith in Christ.

Question to Explore

How can a person
be saved?

Study Aim

To state how a person receives salvation

Study Actions and Emphases

- Share the gospel of Jesus Christ with all people
- Equip people for ministry in the church and in the world

LESSON SEVEN

Good News for Everybody

Quick Read

The early church faced a watershed issue. Do Gentiles need to become Jews if they are to become Christians? The resolution of this question determined whether the early church remained a small sect or set the course for a worldwide movement.

Most Christian congregations face some level of conflict. The sources of the conflict can be many and varied. Doctrinal understanding, biblical interpretation, history and identity, social context, ministry programming, personalities, and how the congregation does its business—each and all can be points of debate.

This lesson demonstrates a model for dealing with such conflict. This model exhibits a protocol for recognizing the essential issues in conflict and finding functional steps for addressing the conflict. Undergirding these ideas, most importantly, is acting on the idea of Christ as Lord. Christlike actions can resolve the conflict and be a witness to the power of the gospel.

Who Should Be Called a Christian? (Acts 11:19–26; 13:44–52; 14:24–28)

This lesson addresses a conflict in the early church. What was necessary for people to be considered a part of the Christian fellowship? As with any contemporary conflict, this one did not occur as a result of only one dynamic. Rather, as today, conflict developed from a variety of patterns and dynamics. Too often we fail to recognize that seemingly unrelated matters actually, from a broader perspective, are related.

Likely, for instance, at least some of the early Christians who knew about the conversion of Cornelius saw it as a somewhat isolated incident. Further, for most, Peter's encounter with Cornelius had little to do with the stress of the persecution of Christians that had developed in Jerusalem. The lesson Acts puts before us is that we must be able to interpret social events that seemingly have little to do with us. Certainly the dynamics underway in the early church were channels by which God's continuing revelation could find expression.

The pattern of persecution can be reviewed as far back as Acts 5 as Jewish leaders reacted harshly out of jealousy over the apostles' success. The stoning of Stephen is described in Acts 7. By Acts 12 we read of the execution of James, brother of John. The times were difficult for those who dared proclaim Jesus as the Lord of life.

Many of the Jews who had become Christians were forced to leave Jerusalem. They traveled north and northwest to escape the harsh treatment. These people traveled to Phoenicia, Cyprus, and Antioch. The pioneers to these places remain nameless. Christians of any era remain in the debt of these and other nameless pioneers of faith.

Acts 15:1–21

¹Then certain individuals came down from Judea and were teaching the brothers, "Unless you are circumcised according to the custom of Moses, you cannot be saved." ²And after Paul and Barnabas had no small dissension and debate with them, Paul and Barnabas and some of the others were appointed to go up to Jerusalem to discuss this question with the apostles and the elders. ³So they were sent on their way by the church, and as they passed through both Phoenicia and Samaria, they reported the conversion of the Gentiles, and brought great joy to all the believers. ⁴When they came to Jerusalem, they were welcomed by the church and the apostles and the elders, and they reported all that God had done with them. ⁵But some believers who belonged to the sect of the Pharisees stood up and said, "It is necessary for them to be circumcised and ordered to keep the law of Moses."

⁶The apostles and the elders met together to consider this matter. ⁷After there had been much debate, Peter stood up and said to them, "My brothers, you know that in the early days God made a choice among you, that I should be the one through whom the Gentiles would hear the message of the good news and become believers. ⁸And God, who knows the human heart, testified to them by giving them the Holy Spirit, just as he did to us; ⁹and in cleansing their hearts by faith he has made no distinction between them and us. ¹⁰Now therefore why are you putting God to the test by placing on the neck of the disciples a yoke that neither our ancestors nor we have been able to bear? ¹¹On the contrary, we believe that we will be saved through the grace of the Lord Jesus, just as they will."

¹²The whole assembly kept silence, and listened to Barnabas and Paul as they told of all the signs and wonders that God had done through them among the Gentiles. ¹³After they finished speaking, James replied, "My brothers, listen to me. ¹⁴Simeon has related how God first looked favorably on the Gentiles, to take from among them a people for his name. ¹⁵This agrees with the words of the prophets, as it is written,

¹⁶ 'After this I will return,
     and I will rebuild the dwelling of David, which has fallen;
     from its ruins I will rebuild it,
     and I will set it up,
¹⁷ so that all other peoples may seek the Lord—
     even all the Gentiles over whom my name has been called.
     Thus says the Lord, who has been making these things ¹⁸known from long ago.'

¹⁹Therefore I have reached the decision that we should not trouble those Gentiles who are turning to God, ²⁰but we should write to them to abstain only from things polluted by idols and from fornication and from whatever has been strangled and from blood. ²¹For in every city, for generations past, Moses has had those who proclaim him, for he has been read aloud every sabbath in the synagogues."

In their new locations, the new Christians began to tell of their faith in Christ. Some of them witnessed only to Jews. Those who arrived in Antioch related the gospel to Hellenists (Acts 11:20). Hellenists were Gentiles. Many responded positively to the gospel.

The news of this response reached Jerusalem. When news of what had happened reached the Jerusalem congregation, they had questions, questions that perhaps indicate disagreement. Perhaps some of their questions were the following: Was it true that Hellenists had received salvation? With no background in Judaism, would these people continue to express their pagan lifestyle and call themselves Christians? How should we as Jewish Christians relate to them?

The believers at Antioch adhered to the ways of Christ so closely that people recognized them by their lifestyle. Do people so recognize us as Christians by how we live?

The concern some of the Jerusalem Christians had indicates a lack of understanding regarding who could become a Christian. It also indicates a high level of provincialism on their part to think that only Jews could become believers. The concern of the Jerusalem Christians further indicates that a rigid legalism was already present in the Christian community.

The decision was made to send someone to gather information. The emissary from Jerusalem to Antioch, no short journey, was Barnabas. This man did not have status as an apostle, but he was a man with stature among the Jerusalem church and beyond. Luke describes him in terms that convey deep integrity. Barnabas was "a good man, full of the Holy Spirit and of faith" (11:24).

What Barnabas found was the movement of the Holy Spirit among the Christians of Antioch. Barnabas encouraged these people. Also, he went to get Saul (Paul) in Tarsus, further northwest of Antioch. Then, together Barnabas and Saul set to work educating these new Christians toward maturity in their faith. These two remained at this task for a year. The

Hellenists

Hellene is another word for a Greek. The term was used in the New Testament to describe anyone who had adopted the Greek lifestyle. Greek culture was marked by the city-state form of government, an empirical approach to life, and highly developed arts and literature. Intellectualism, militarism, and athletics also characterized the culture.

The Greek culture can be traced at least 500 years before the New Testament era. Its broadest development came with the conquests of Philip of Macedon and his son Alexander the Great. They conquered the known world 350 years before the New Testament era. The culture was so imposing the Romans adopted it wholesale upon their conquest of the Greeks. Western civilization, to our day, can trace its style of government, philosophy, arts, and sciences to the Hellenists.

---

level of commitment on their part toward developing the Christian education of the Antioch Christians is inspirational. Note that Barnabas did not report immediately back to Jerusalem, as if somehow the Jerusalem church were in charge of the Christian movement. Barnabas' actions tend to affirm our Baptist approach of congregational church government.

Luke did add a noteworthy comment in 11:26. The followers of Christ were *first* called Christians in Antioch. That remark alone should have persuaded the detractors about the Christians in Antioch. The believers at Antioch adhered to the ways of Christ so closely that people recognized them by their lifestyle. Do people so recognize us as Christians by how we live?

> *Christians' egos and sense of pseudo-superiority can blind them to what God is really doing.*

In Acts 13:44–52, Luke adds another narrative depicting further reactions to Gentile Christians. By this time, the Antioch Christians had commissioned Paul and Barnabas to extend their work to other locations. Thus, what is known as the first missionary journey of Paul began. The team embarked to Cyprus, crossed the island where they established new work, and then went back to the mainland. There they journeyed north to another Antioch, Antioch of Pisidia.

At this place, the issue of what is involved in experiencing the salvation of God came to a head. The response to Paul and Barnabas was mixed. Luke said, "almost the whole city gathered" to hear them. When Paul and Barnabas made the claim that God had sent light to the Gentiles, the Gentiles in the audience affirmed them. Many of the Gentiles also became Christian believers. The Jewish leaders, however, countered this concept and stirred many in the crowd against Paul and Barnabas. The crowd forced them out of town. However, these early evangelists responded with a sense of joy over the obvious work of the Holy Spirit among Gentiles.

In Acts 14:24–28, Luke related the conclusion of the first missionary trip. Paul and Barnabas made their way back to their starting place, Antioch (in Syria). This was a time of reporting and likely some recuperation. These men had traveled an extraordinary distance, visited an incredible number of people, and spent a huge amount of energy proclaiming and teaching the gospel, establishing new churches, and offering encouragement wherever they went. Paul and Barnabas happily related their experiences of verifying God's movement among the Gentiles.

Too often, contemporary Christians fail the test of relating to anyone who sincerely names Jesus as Lord.

Thus, Luke built the case for his readers. The Christian movement had covered an enormous amount of territory. A large number of people had been persuaded to believe in Christ. Trusted Christian leaders had given personal testimony of the power of the gospel in the lives of Gentiles as well as Jews. So there should be no doubt that Gentiles could experience the redeeming grace of God through Jesus Christ. Controversy continued to exist, however.

Detractors and Exclusivists (Acts 15:1–5)

The time for encouragement from and toward Paul and Barnabas was short lived. Such is the cycle in church life some times. The insightful church member will watch for such cycles. Whenever a strongly held position is challenged, those holding that position can be expected to respond.

Those who could be called Judaizers played the role of spoilers of the good things at Antioch. The spirit of Christian freedom in relationships between the former Jews and Gentiles who had become Christians was unthinkable for the Judaizers. For these people, one had to become a Jew before he or she could become a Christian.

We might find such a thought rather foolish. People in our time, however, continue to have different kinds of hoops for people to jump through to prove their worth and place in a Christian congregation. Sometimes these criteria are written out. Sometimes they remain unspoken.

Paul and Barnabas, as we would expect, debated with these detractors and exclusivists. The argument was heated. Paul and Barnabas were able to give firsthand accounts of the validity of Gentile conversions. Likely the Judaizers feared that immoral practices held over from Hellenistic cultic practice could be brought into Christian congregations through these Gentiles.

When no resolution could be reached in Antioch, the decision was made for Paul, Barnabas, and evidently people representing the different positions to go to Jerusalem. One might read into this decision an appeal made to a higher level of a hierarchy. Perhaps, however, we should consider the trip to Jerusalem to be more of an appeal to those who had more wisdom and more objectivity.

Although we will not become free of conflict, we can learn to exhibit how to deal with conflict constructively.

On the way to Jerusalem, the reports from Paul and Barnabas were met with enthusiasm. The character of this enthusiasm helps us realize that other Christians shared the view of Gentile conversion that Paul and Barnabas held. Note that certain church leaders could not accept the action of God, but ordinary believers could.

Again Paul and Barnabas had to endure criticism. Like parentheses around the heart of a matter, verses one and five recount the cry that the Gentile believers had to be circumcised and keep the law of Moses to be Christians.

Luke described the Jerusalem critics as "some believers who belonged to the sect of the Pharisees" (15:5). Likely these believers were attempting to maintain a "pure" line of Christianity, probably a high motive. Still they failed to see their shortsightedness. Their attitude and actions indicate that even believers with high motives can miss expressing the grace, freedom, and openness to which the gospel calls us. Christians' egos and sense of pseudo-superiority can blind them to what God is really doing.

What *IS* God Up To? (Acts 15:6–11)

The issues were not so clear-cut to those who heard the arguments from the Judaizers on one side and Paul and Barnabas on the other. The larger discussion was relatively new. The test cases were just showing up. Some confusion was involved. So the debate continued.

Then Peter arose to speak (15:6). Was it Peter's stature in this group, his clearly stated rationale, or both that put the issue in stark relief? Whichever, the reader can sense the emotion and energy of the discussion shifting.

> *We can demonstrate to a larger world, deeply entrenched in destructive conflict, some beneficial ways to be reconciled.*

Peter's points were simple. He recognized that God had recruited him (15:7). He had not initiated the gospel witness to Cornelius and his household. The conversions were authentic and reflected the same elements as those in the group around him (15:8). Peter was convinced there were no criteria that should be employed to make the Gentiles' salvation inferior or more strenuous (15:9–11). Even the Judaizers could not carry the yoke of the law they wanted to require the Gentile believers to carry!

Peter's final comment is as fine a distillation of what salvation in Christ is and how it comes as is found in the New Testament: "We believe that we will be saved through the grace of the Lord Jesus, just as they will" (15:10).

How, Then, Do We Live? (Acts 15:12–20)

The silence that followed Peter's remarks spoke volumes. It was a signal that something was about to be decided.

James, a half-brother of Jesus, was likely the convener of this group. He spoke next. He consolidated the discussion with reference to Peter, whom

Inclusive or Exclusive?

Contemporary Christians talk about the inclusiveness of God's grace. At the same time, Christian congregations sometimes function as some of the most exclusive organizations in our society.

- In what ways do churches sometimes express exclusiveness? (For example, certain people are not asked to serve in positions of leadership.)
- Are your congregation's guidelines for exclusion and inclusion more related to the tenets of the gospel or to your congregation's cultural understandings?
- How do you think Barnabas, Paul, and Peter would respond to these cultural understandings?

he identified by Peter's Hebrew name—Simeon. Next, James noted the correlation of Peter's experience with what the prophet Amos had said centuries before (Amos 9:11–12). James was wise enough to note that the quibbling over whether to relate to Gentile believers should be understood in respect to the larger revelation of God.

To the credit of James, the decision was made to work with Gentile believers and to encourage Gentile conversion. Some moral guidelines were put before the Hellenist Christians, though. These guidelines should not be read as something extra for the Hellenistic believers to do. Rather, being new to the faith and surrounded by a culture that promoted lifestyles alien to Christianity, they needed to educate themselves and act with moral responsibility. These same considerations were expected of the Judaizers. Moral accountability was no higher or lower for any group.

The pattern of the New Testament church demonstrates that the good news is for everyone.

These guidelines constituted some functional bases put forward for the alienated groups to use in order to work together. Trust could replace suspicion. Civility could replace incivility. Acceptance could overturn alienation. Cooperation could replace disjointed and half-hearted endeavors.

The guidelines from James remained just that for some of the group known as the Judaizers. A quick scan of the rest of Acts and the Pauline epistles reveals that the Judaizers were ever present, countering the preaching and teaching of Paul and the others (see the Book of Galatians, especially).

These detractors continued attempting to impose further regulations and standards for what it meant to be redeemed. Their behavior demonstrated a lack of peace and a spirit of reconciliation (marks of the presence of God) within them.

What was at stake in the Jerusalem Council were such issues as these:

(1) What is necessary for Christian conversion?

(2) How are Christians of various cultures and backgrounds to relate to one another?

Hardly a church has avoided something like the conflict that went on between Jerusalem and Antioch and beyond. Too often, contemporary Christians fail the test of relating to anyone who sincerely names Jesus as Lord.

Conflict about something will probably be a given in contemporary Christian circles. A conflict free congregation will never exist. We must make a part of our Christian efforts the identification of what kind of conflict we have, however, and begin to address that conflict.

Is it any wonder that the larger society is confused about Christianity? So many different messages are communicated from Christian entities, often with each characterized as portraying the will of God. We hear the words *grace, reconciliation,* and *fellowship* from denominations, congregations, and individual Christians. Yet, relationships between Christians often are marked by jealousy, resentment, bigotry, and outright hatred. We sometimes extend, unfortunately, more bad news than we do the good news of the gospel of Jesus Christ.

We can do better, and we must. Although we will not become free of conflict, we can learn to exhibit how to deal with conflict constructively. We can actually grow and mature through conflict. Conflict can become our tool, not our master, toward expressing the power of the gospel. We can demonstrate to a larger world, deeply entrenched in destructive conflict, some beneficial ways to be reconciled. This reconciliation can occur as we let our values and actions be informed and formed through a living relationship with the living Lord Jesus Christ.

The pattern of the New Testament church demonstrates that the good news *is* for everyone. It also shows us that there are resources for extending the gospel in that way.

QUESTIONS

1. Do some congregations and Christians put more weight on being a member of the "right" church than on what it means to be a Christian? What are some ways this perspective is expressed?

2. How would you respond to this statement: *Congregations today fail to express the gospel clearly because they have not experienced persecution as did the first-century Christians.*

3. What are some spoken or written criteria we use to authenticate a person's profession that he or she is a Christian?

4. What are some of the marks of God moving among people?

5. Can you develop a way of dealing with congregational conflict from this lesson? (For example: identifying the issue(s) and value(s) in question; gathering information; recognizing cultural dynamics informing the conflict; considering where the movement of God is, though all positions may claim to have "the mind of God on the matter"; identifying plans of action.) Fill in details that would fit your congregation.

UNIT

Interpreting the Meaning of Jesus
3

Unit 3, "Interpreting the Meaning of Jesus," continues the emphasis on Jesus of earlier units by showing how Jesus enters into and influences our everyday lives. Certainly this title represents the nature of the entire New Testament. The meaning of Jesus for our everyday lives constitutes the primary focus of every section of the Testament.

Each of this unit's six lessons comes from a different book in the New Testament. The nature of these books is different from that of the gospels or Acts. The kinds of literature for these lessons are epistles (Romans, 2 Corinthians, Hebrews, 1 John, and 2 Peter) and apocalyptic literature, The Revelation of John. Apocalyptic literature is a special type of biblical writing. This type of literature is designed to communicate to people whose culture and training allow them to understand while the meaning remains hidden to others without these special insights.

The six lessons in the unit present a wonderful progression in the Christian life. Lesson eight focuses on chapter 8 of Paul's Epistle to the Romans. The lesson demonstrates how the Holy Spirit empowers those in Christ to maintain an intimate relationship with God and to face life's difficulties with confidence and assurance. Lesson nine, from 2 Corinthians 4—5, indicates how those who have this relationship with God in Christ share in Christ's ministry to others and selflessly call others to be reconciled with God in Christ.

The tenth lesson, based on Hebrews 11:1—12:17, considers the nature of faith and how we are to demonstrate our faith. This lesson teaches that belief in Christ brings a person into a relationship with God that inspires him or her to live faithfully and perform for God those works that cannot be done without faith.

Lesson eleven, from 1 John 4:7–21, points to love as the very heart of the gospel of Christ. Those in Christ, said the Apostle John, will love both God and others because love is the essence of God's nature. The lesson from 2 Peter 3:3–15 (lesson twelve) not only tells of the promise of the second coming of Christ but also shows how those who believe in this coming should behave in light of this promise.

The final lesson in the unit (lesson thirteen), from Revelation 5, is meant to climax the study by pointing directly to Christ, our Redeemer. This lesson emphasizes that Christ, the Lamb of God, is worthy of all praise and honor.

These lessons carry us through the meaning of new life in Christ, ministry in Christ's name, faithfulness in his service, love through his example, behavior in light of his promised coming, and praise due to the fact that Christ and Christ alone is worthy of all praise and honor. This unit on the meaning of Jesus for life today could well be a highlight of your spiritual journey![1]

UNIT THREE: INTERPRETING THE MEANING OF JESUS

Lesson 8	New Life in Christ	Romans 8:1–17, 31–39
Lesson 9	Selfless Ministry for Christ	2 Corinthians 4:7–11; 5:11–21
Lesson 10	A Faith That Means Faithfulness	Hebrews 11:1–2, 8–28, 32—12:3
Lesson 11	Love, the Heart of the Gospel	1 John 4:7–21
Lesson 12	The Promise of His Coming	2 Peter 3:3–15*a*
Lesson 13	Worthy Is the Lamb	Revelation 5

NOTES

1. Unless otherwise indicated, all Scripture quotes in Unit 3, Lessons 8–13, are from the New Revised Standard Version.

Focal Text

Romans 8:1–17, 31–39

Background

Romans 8

Main Idea

When we are in Christ, the Spirit empowers us to live in an intimate, faithful relationship with God our Father and thus to face life's difficulties with confidence.

Question to Explore

What difference does Christ make for you today?

Study Aim

To tell how Christ makes a difference in our lives, in both blessings and responsibilities

Study Actions and Emphases

- Share the gospel of Jesus Christ with all people
- Equip people for ministry in the church and in the world
- Develop Christian families
- Strengthen existing churches and start new congregations

LESSON EIGHT

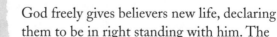

New Life in Christ

Quick Read

God freely gives believers new life, declaring them to be in right standing with him. The Holy Spirit empowers these believers to live in intimate relationship with God as God's children and face life's difficulties with hope, assurance, and security.

The entire community looked down on Bob (not his name) because he seemed to be handicapped. He wore clothes that were ragged and often almost embarrassing. I tried to witness to him, but he did not respond. The people in the community advised I not try to help him. They thought he was too handicapped to respond.

After God had moved me to another place of service, several years later I was invited to return to the church to speak. A young man sat on the back row. He was neat, well groomed, and at ease. After the service he asked me whether I remembered him. I admitted I did not know who he was. He told me he was that same man who used to seem so handicapped.

What had happened? He had become a Christian. God had given him new life in Christ, and the Holy Spirit had empowered him to practice the Christian life. This lesson considers the new life that comes through faith in Jesus Christ.

Romans 8 declares that God gives Christians a new and different kind of life in Christ. The Holy Spirit empowers believers to live in intimate relationship with God through the freedom Christ gives. Believers' new status in Christ assures them that they are: (1) accepted by God (free from condemnation); (2) allowed to live as children of God; (3) enabled to face difficulties with hope; and (4) given assurance that they will never be separated from God. Life in Christ promises Christians that life has new meaning, new strength, new service, and new value. In this new life the Spirit continuously empowers our experiences and ministries.

The Message of Romans for Christians Today

The theme of Paul's Letter to the Romans is that the gospel is the power of God to provide salvation, the God-kind of righteousness (right standing with God) to all people (1:16–17). All people, Paul said, need this right standing that only God provides. All people—both the Gentiles (1:18–32) and the Jews (2:1—3:20)—stand without excuse before God. Having established this universal need, Paul taught that the gospel reveals God's way of making people right in his presence (3:21—6:23). Chapter 7, which may reflect Paul's own experience, leads directly to chapter 8. In Romans 8, the apostle described the new life in Christ (8:1–39). The final sections of the letter deal with the situation of the Jewish people and their relationship to this gospel (9:1—11:36) and call for commitment to the ethical requirements of the Christian Faith (12:1—16:27).

Romans 8:1–17, 31–39

1There is therefore now no condemnation for those who are in Christ Jesus. 2For the law of the Spirit of life in Christ Jesus has set you free from the law of sin and of death. 3For God has done what the law, weakened by the flesh, could not do: by sending his own Son in the likeness of sinful flesh, and to deal with sin, he condemned sin in the flesh, 4so that the just requirement of the law might be fulfilled in us, who walk not according to the flesh but according to the Spirit. 5For those who live according to the flesh set their minds on the things of the flesh, but those who live according to the Spirit set their minds on the things of the Spirit. 6To set the mind on the flesh is death, but to set the mind on the Spirit is life and peace. 7For this reason the mind that is set on the flesh is hostile to God; it does not submit to God's law—indeed it cannot, 8and those who are in the flesh cannot please God.

9But you are not in the flesh; you are in the Spirit, since the Spirit of God dwells in you. Anyone who does not have the Spirit of Christ does not belong to him. 10But if Christ is in you, though the body is dead because of sin, the Spirit is life because of righteousness. 11If the Spirit of him who raised Jesus from the dead dwells in you, he who raised Christ from the dead will give life to your mortal bodies also through his Spirit that dwells in you.

12So then, brothers and sisters, we are debtors, not to the flesh, to live according to the flesh—13for if you live according to the flesh, you will die; but if by the Spirit you put to death the deeds of the body, you will live. 14For all who are led by the Spirit of God are children of God. 15For you did not receive a spirit of slavery to fall back into fear, but you have received a spirit of adoption. When we cry, "Abba! Father!" 16it is that very Spirit bearing witness with our spirit that we are children of God, 17and if children, then heirs, heirs of God and joint heirs with Christ—if, in fact, we suffer with him so that we may also be glorified with him.

• •

31What then are we to say about these things? If God is for us, who is against us? 32He who did not withhold his own Son, but gave him up for all of us, will he not with him also give us everything else? 33Who will bring any charge against God's elect? It is God who justifies. 34Who is to condemn? It is Christ Jesus, who died, yes, who was raised, who is at the right hand of God, who indeed intercedes for us. 35Who will separate us from the love of Christ? Will hardship, or distress, or persecution, or famine, or nakedness, or peril, or sword? 36As it is written,

> "For your sake we are being killed all day long;
> we are accounted as sheep to be slaughtered."
> [37]No, in all these things we are more than conquerors through him who loved us. [38]For I am convinced that neither death, nor life, nor angels, nor rulers, nor things present, nor things to come, nor powers, [39]nor height, nor depth, nor anything else in all creation, will be able to separate us from the love of God in Christ Jesus our Lord.

Chapter 8, the focus of our study, ushers us from the almost starless night of struggle in chapter 7 to the dawn of hope in Christ. The beauty and majesty of this chapter has been described by saying that if the Scriptures were a ring, and the Epistle to the Romans the precious gem, then chapter 8 would be the sparkling point of the jewel. Paul testifies to the glory of new life in Christ, which frees believers to live in God's way and avoid the pitfalls of the flesh.

More references to the Holy Spirit exist in Romans 8 than in any other chapter of Paul's letters. God's grace bestows the new life in Christ. The Spirit empowers believers to practice fully the Christian life.

Empowered for Victory Over Sin and Death (8:1–13)

The word "therefore" in 8:1 conveys this thought: *the conclusion of the matter is this*. Because deliverance is now available in Christ, believers no longer need to continue in servitude. The law of Christ has freed them from the bondage to law. There is "now" no condemnation (8:1). Believers stand acquitted from the sentence against them and are set free from the enslaving power of sin and the law principle that caused them to strive to create right standing with God on their own.

The Holy Spirit empowers believers to live in intimate relationship with God through the freedom Christ gives.

The old principle of sin and death shows the impossibility of living out God's law and will (7:14–21). The old principle reduces people to despair (7:24). New life in Christ breaks the dominance of the life of sin and death and empowers believers to experience intimate relationship with God and victory in Jesus.

The way this wonderful victory is achieved appears in 8:3–4. The law could not break the power of sin and death because it was weak. It had to work through fallen human nature. God, by sending his Son, Jesus Christ, as a sin offering, broke the power of sin and brought its authority to an end. The demands of the law, which could not be fulfilled by unredeemed humans, can now be attained by those who are walking in the Spirit. By his death, Christ voided and expelled the sin that had invaded humanity.

Paul did not mean that people who were empowered by the Spirit were enabled to be saved by keeping the law. Such would be justification by works. The teaching is that now, in Christ, believers can keep the requirements of the law. Working from within, the Spirit motivates and empowers believers to behavior that the law could never impel them to follow. Christians become unwilling to continue in deliberate sin.

> *Life in Christ promises Christians that life has new meaning, new strength, new service, and new value.*

In 8:5–12, Paul contrasted the old life that was ruled and controlled by the flesh (lower nature) with the new life in Christ that is guided and empowered by the Spirit. This empowering comes by the fact that believers are "in the Spirit" and "the Spirit of God dwells in" them (8:9).

Those who have experienced deliverance (8:1–11) have no obligation to live according to the desires of the old sinful nature. Paul further indicates that if a person lives by the flesh—that is, in conformity to the

The Letter to the Romans

The influence and spiritual value of the Letter to the Romans is profound and immeasurable. The Holy Spirit used this epistle as an instrument in the salvation experiences of Augustine, Martin Luther, and John Wesley, among many. Indeed, Luther declared that Romans could not be read too often. The more one tastes the words the more delicious they become. Some call Romans Paul's *magnum opus* and the single most complete expression of the missionary message.

Paul was probably in Corinth when he penned the epistle to "all God's beloved in Rome" who had been "called to be saints" (Romans 1:7). These Christians most likely were gathered into many small, diverse congregations that reflected the cultural mix of this vast urban setting. Paul addressed these differing groups, some Jewish, some Gentile, with a letter designed to set forth systematically the message as the inspired apostle understood it. Since Paul had not started the Roman congregations, he may have desired to clarify to them his understanding of the Christian faith—perhaps partly to secure their support for his intended missionary effort in Spain.

desires of the lower nature—the person will die. But one who treats as dead "the deeds of the body" will live (8:13). The meaning literally is that the person *keeps on* putting to death or mortifying the "*mis*deeds of the body."

Mortifying or putting to death the misdeeds of the body is not something a person can do by his or her own moral power. Such human effort is doomed, just as the efforts of those who sought to attain right standing with God by observing the Jewish law were doomed. The act of putting to death the flesh can only be realized by the divine working as one allows the Spirit to "put to death" the carnal nature (8:13).

> New life in Christ breaks the dominance of the life of sin and death and empowers believers to experience intimate relationship with God and victory in Jesus.

The Holy Spirit empowers believers to walk in the new life in Christ, thus enabling them to reach victory over sin and death. The same Spirit allows believers to become and behave like children of God.

Empowered to Become Children and Heirs of God (8:14–17)

Verse 14 asserts that those and only those who are habitually, continually, and progressively being led by God's Spirit are actually the children of God. Two ideas run throughout this paragraph—sonship and heirship. Sonship points to the believer's present relationship with God; heirship to the promise of our future glorious relationship. New life in Christ assures believers of both.

Verse 14 further teaches that our obedient following of Christ gives evidence of our relationship with God. This sonship in action is a more dependable indicator of salvation than emotional highs or lows. This obedient walk constitutes a paramount test of our relationship with God.

The Enabling Spirit

The Holy Spirit empowers Christians to:
(1) attain victory over sin and death (8:1–13)
(2) become children and heirs of God (8:14–17)
(3) exercise hope in God's care when facing trials (8:18–30)
(4) rest in the assurance of God's eternal security (8:31–39)

The word "spirit" in verse 15 refers to the human spirit, not to God's Holy Spirit. Paul said that when a person is conscious of sonship, he or she no longer has a "spirit" of fear or slavery. Such a spirit is a person's state under the law. Under the law, one abides in constant fear of not fulfilling that law. But those who have received the "spirit of adoption" have the consciousness of being adopted sons with freedom to address God as father (8:15).

Two beautiful terms in 8:15, "adoption" and "Abba," testify to the wonder of salvation. Paul teaches that sonship through adoption gives believers a profound sense of assurance.

The term, "Abba," an Aramaic word, was the intimate term by which a Jewish child addressed the father. Of the times the New Testament uses the term, two are in Pauline letters (Rom. 8:15; Galatians 4:6). The third use occurs in Jesus' Gethsemane prayer to the Father (Mark 14:36). The term expresses a warm, trusting, personal, certain relationship between Jesus and the Father.

Romans 8:16 speaks of the assurance of sonship or relationship by saying that the Holy Spirit bears consistent witness with our human spirit that we are indeed children of God. The Holy Spirit endorses our inward conviction that we are children of God. The Spirit speaks to us deep in our hearts and tells us we are God's children.

The "if" clause in verse 17 expresses a reality. It could be translated *and if, as we assuredly are, children of God*. It testifies to the reality of Christians' God-given sonship. Paul used both the term for sons (8:14) and the term for children (vs. 16–17), perhaps to indicate that both males and females are included. As adopted children, believers have full rights of family membership. While we will be heirs with Christ, we have not yet fully received the inheritance. It remains in the future. While

The Holy Spirit empowers believers to walk in the new life in Christ, thus enabling them to reach victory over sin and death.

we have full assurance of future glory, we still experience strain, suffering, and opposition. As we share the suffering brought on by following Christ we will also share in Christ's ultimate glory. The phrase "if, in fact, we suffer with him," like the previous *if* clause, assumes reality. It can be translated, *if, as is the case, we share in his sufferings*.

Romans 8:14–17 testifies of the reality and assurance of sonship in the Christian life. Believers are assured of guidance by the Spirit, of power to overcome sin, of freedom to approach God, and of certainty of receiving

Christ's glory. The next section of the letter shows that the believer's status in Christ gives hope, comfort, and assurance in the face of sufferings or hardships.

Empowered to Hope in the Face of Suffering (8:18–30)

Paul sought to encourage believers in the midst of the sufferings they would experience as followers of Christ. He pointed to the surpassing greatness of the future glory that far exceeds the present sufferings (8:18). Creation will share in the coming glory even though it has been under the domination of human sinfulness (8:19–22). As the creation groans, awaiting the full redemption in Christ, so believers look forward in the hope of the full redemption of the body (8:23–25). Hope, in the biblical sense, represents an assurance, not a *perhaps* or only a possible desire.

> *The Spirit speaks to us deep in our hearts and tells us we are God's children.*

Believers can rest assured that the Spirit will continue helping according to the promises of God (8:26–30). The Spirit helps with prayer, interceding on our behalf even when we do not know for what we should pray (8:26–27). Furthermore, God makes "all things" work together for the good of his people (8:28). This wonderful promise does not mean that believers face no trials or sufferings. Rather, it means that when we trust our experiences to God, God creates good out of even our worst experiences. All of God's blessings come about because of the eternal purpose of God to bring these blessings (8:29–30).

These divine promises bring to the believer an absolute assurance of eternal security. This teaching is the subject of the letter's next section.

Empowered to Practice the Assurance of Security (8:31–39)

Believers can not only believe in the assurance of salvation but can actually live out this belief in practice. Romans 8:31–39 uses several unanswerable questions to testify to the solid foundation of Christian confidence and assurance. All of these questions grow out of the affirmation of God's unchanging, invincible purpose and are designed to give believers a deep sense of spiritual security. In life and in death the Christian has assurance of absolute security.

The Meaning of Adoption

It was a frightening, anxious day at the elementary school. Parents were frantic, teachers stressed, children in panic. One teacher, new to the community, had the trying task of enrolling the children who were new to the school. As she enrolled the children, she realized that the skinny, tow-headed boy in front of her had given the same last name, the same address, and the same parents' names as a young fellow a few minutes earlier. His birthday, though, was only five months different.

The teacher said, "I thought I just enrolled a boy with the last name, address, and parents the same as yours, but you are only five months older than he is."

The boy answered with a slightly puzzled look, "Oh, yeah, that was my brother! One of us is adopted, but I can't remember which it is."

It's a great thing to be adopted! It means a family in a special way goes out to invite a child to become a member of the family. Parents who have both adopted and naturally born children acknowledge that they feel and show equal love and care for adopted and naturally born offspring.

When the Holy Spirit led Paul to describe what it meant to become a Christian, one of the words Paul was led to use was adoption. Adoption refers to being brought into the family of God with all the advantages and privileges of sonship. Christians become children and heirs of God—joint heirs with Christ in God's Kingdom.

First, believers' security finds foundation in God's gracious action on their behalf (8:31–32). Since God is on our side, who can be against us? Perhaps a better translation is, *Since God is on our side, what does it matter who is against us?* But what gives us certainty that God is for us? Nothing less than the cross! Calvary marks God's great commitment to us (see 5:6–11). The phrase "gave him up" emphasizes the sheer goodness of the divine gift (8:32).

Believers are assured of guidance by the Spirit, of power to overcome sin, of freedom to approach God, and of certainty of receiving Christ's glory.

Second, believers' security finds foundation in God's acquittal of the sinner and Christ's continuing intercession (8:33–34). The verses picture a courtroom where God acquits and no one can bring further charges. It is Christ himself who pronounces the Christian to be right with God. Further, no one can condemn us. Christ is at the right hand of the Father, interceding for Christians. The dying Christ, resurrected and ascended to heaven, continually pleads the cause of believers.

Third, believers' security rests on the truth that God's great love will prevent anything from separating Christians from their Lord (8:35–39). In 8:35, Paul mentioned seven fearful threats that cannot come between believers and God. While these threats could appear terrifying, Paul affirmed that in all of these dangers, Christians are "more than conquerors through him who loved us" (8:37; literally, *they keep on gloriously conquering or win an overwhelming victory through the one who loved us*). Verse 37 is one of Scripture's greatest affirmations of faith.

> In life and in death the Christian has assurance of absolute security.

The apostle was absolutely "convinced" (8:38) that nothing in all creation could separate believers from God's love in Christ. "Neither death, nor life" can intervene in or take away the believers' relationship with God. Neither "angels" (messengers from heaven) "nor rulers" can separate a believer from his or her Lord. The word translated "rulers" is sometimes viewed as an earthly ruler or monarch and sometimes as a supernatural, demonic being. Paul used the word in both senses in his writings. The word "powers" usually carried the meaning of supernatural, evil powers. My own understanding is that the first word, translated "rulers," refers in this verse to earthly powers and that the second word, translated "powers," relates to evil, supernatural powers. Thus, death, life, angels, monarchs, or superhuman foes cannot separate Christians from God.

Paul was equally convinced that no uncertainty in the present world or in the coming world ("nor things present, nor things to come") would come between believers and God (8:38–39). Neither will any power from on high (above) nor from below remove believers from the Lord's presence. Nothing has power to separate Christians from God's love in Christ. Clearly, the apostle affirmed that God's love in Christ brings to the Christian victory and assurance in the face of any and every foe.

Believers rest assured that their salvation, which comes by Christ, will be completed by Christ. Those who are truly saved will endure to the end. That is, they will never be lost again.

Conclusion

New life in Christ brings to the believer a completely new existence. The Holy Spirit brings Christians into a new and intimate relationship with

God and empowers them to prevail over sin and death, to live as children of God, to maintain hope in trials, and to demonstrate the assurance of eternal security.

Accept the truth of new life in Christ and the difference it can make in you. Give the Spirit full freedom to dwell in you and empower you to relationship with God and service to others.

QUESTIONS

1. What difference has Christ made in your life since you became a believer? What further changes do you think you should allow Christ to make in you?

2. Are you comfortable in an intimate relationship with God through Christ? List truths from this study that might help you develop such intimacy and trust.

3. Do you sometimes feel guilty because of sinful actions or thoughts in your life? What does Romans 8:1–8 teach about what God has done to free you from this guilt?

4. Are you anxious or fearful? Are you terrified of some seen or unseen possibility? In light of Romans 8:35–39, do you need to be fearful?

5. What does a good parent (father, mother) do for his or her children? Will God not do even more for you than a parent will or can do for a child? What does this truth mean for your life?

6. When difficult times come, what assurances does Romans 8:28 provide?

7. What evidence do you see of God's continuing love and care for you?

8. Why do true believers never need to fear they will lose God's salvation?

Focal Text

2 Corinthians 4:7–11;
5:11–21

Background

2 Corinthians 4—5

Main Idea

Because God has
reconciled us to himself
through Christ, we are
to share the message
of reconciliation with
others in a spirit of
humble trust in God.

Questions to Explore

In what spirit do you
serve Christ and share his
message? Or do you?

Study Aim

To describe the spirit in which we are to serve
Christ and share Christ's message

Study and Action Emphases

- Share the gospel of Jesus Christ with all
  people
- Minister to human needs in the name of
  Jesus Christ
- Equip people for ministry in the church
  and in the world

LESSON NINE

Selfless Ministry for Christ

Quick Read

God in Christ reconciles believers to himself
and gives believers the ministry of reconciliation
in which they call others to reconciliation.

Have you known people who produce discord and conflict in every situation and with every group they associate? Usually, these people sow discord and conflict because they are not happy with themselves. Due to low self-image, they feel others do not love or accept them and act so as to cause that exact reaction.

On the other hand, perhaps you know people who bring into every relationship peace and reconciliation. To become such a peacemaker, one must be *at one* with God, with self, and therefore able to be *at one* with others.

This lesson deals with the process of becoming *at one*, that is in right relationship with God, self, and others through becoming right with God. Jesus, by his death on the cross, has made it possible for sin to be canceled and believers brought into right relationship with God. Paul used a Greek word translated *to reconcile*. The word means *to cause to be friendly or harmonious again*. God in Christ brings the sinful person back into harmonious relationship with himself. Being at one with God, the forgiven believer can then help others be reconciled to God, to themselves, and to others. This peace-making life is the ministry of reconciliation that can be realized only through selfless service to God and others.

In 2 Corinthians 4—5 Paul challenged us to give ourselves to the selfless ministry of healing broken relationships—first and foremost to bridging broken relationships between people and God but also reconciling people to one another. Believers should join with Christ in this glorious ministry of renewing proper relationships between people and God and between people and others. The gospel of Jesus Christ, different from the message of the old law, makes this reconciliation possible. A major segment of 2 Corinthians relates to the subject for this lesson, "Selfless Ministry for Christ," to which the apostle calls all believers. In the focal passage we learn clearly of the nature of this selfless ministry—the ministry of reconciliation.

Power for the Ministry of Reconciliation (2 Cor. 4:7–11)

In 2 Corinthians 3:1—4:6, Paul described the splendor of the gospel. Paul declared that the nature of the gospel and the power for its proclamation stem totally and solely from God who in Christ was and is bringing people into right relationship with himself.

Second Corinthians 4:7–11 is tied closely to 3:1—4:6. Paul's boldness to proclaim the gospel message rested on his confidence in God's power and

2 Corinthians 4:7–11

[7]But we have this treasure in clay jars, so that it may be made clear that this extraordinary power belongs to God and does not come from us. [8]We are afflicted in every way, but not crushed; perplexed, but not driven to despair; [9]persecuted, but not forsaken; struck down, but not destroyed; [10]always carrying in the body the death of Jesus, so that the life of Jesus may also be made visible in our bodies. [11]For while we live, we are always being given up to death for Jesus' sake, so that the life of Jesus may be made visible in our mortal flesh.

2 Corinthians 5:11–21

[11]Therefore, knowing the fear of the Lord, we try to persuade others; but we ourselves are well known to God, and I hope that we are also well known to your consciences. [12]We are not commending ourselves to you again, but giving you an opportunity to boast about us, so that you may be able to answer those who boast in outward appearance and not in the heart. [13]For if we are beside ourselves, it is for God; if we are in our right mind, it is for you. [14]For the love of Christ urges us on, because we are convinced that one has died for all; therefore all have died. [15]And he died for all, so that those who live might live no longer for themselves, but for him who died and was raised for them.

[16]From now on, therefore, we regard no one from a human point of view; even though we once knew Christ from a human point of view, we know him no longer in that way. [17]So if anyone is in Christ, there is a new creation: everything old has passed away; see, everything has become new! [18]All this is from God, who reconciled us to himself through Christ, and has given us the ministry of reconciliation; [19]that is, in Christ God was reconciling the world to himself, not counting their trespasses against them, and entrusting the message of reconciliation to us. [20]So we are ambassadors for Christ, since God is making his appeal through us; we entreat you on behalf of Christ, be reconciled to God. [21]For our sake he made him to be sin who knew no sin, so that in him we might become the righteousness of God.

the truth of the life-giving Spirit (3:4–6). This message, the new covenant in Christ, was vastly superior to the old covenant, which condemned the law-breaker without giving any power to make him or her right with God. Because of Paul's confidence in the gospel, he served with boldness.

Paul declared we have "this ministry" (4:1), that is, the new covenant that is the work of the Spirit, in liberty, freedom, and power

Paul's Letters to the Corinthians

The city of Corinth marked the location for one of Paul's most effective ministries (see Acts 18:1–18). He planted Christianity in Corinth on his second missionary journey in AD 50.

Christians in Corinth lived in a secular, sensuous, sinful environment in which the people were obsessed with pleasure, affluence, and sexual misconduct. While at Ephesus on his third missionary journey, Paul heard reports of sinful living that had erupted among believers. Paul sought to correct these problems by writing letters to the Corinthian Christians.

The apostle heard from "Chloe's people" of divisions in Corinth (1 Corinthians 1: 11), indications of sexual immorality (1 Cor. 5:1), and a list of questions from the Corinthians (1 Cor. 7:1; 8:1; 12:1; 16:1). Paul evidently wrote an earlier letter from Ephesus giving instructions not to associate with immoral people (1 Cor. 5:9–11). In response to news from Corinth and the subsequent visit of other Corinthian leaders, Paul wrote 1 Corinthians. He dealt with numerous problems in that letter.

Crisis continued in Corinth, causing Paul to visit the Christians. His visit was short and painful (2 Cor. 2:1). It is unrecorded in Acts. The apostle referred to a letter in which he called for discipline of the wrongdoer in Corinth (see 2 Cor. 2:3–9; 7:8–12). This "severe" letter is lost unless, as some contend, it is preserved as 2 Corinthians 10—13. The "severe" letter seems to have had the desired result. Paul received a good report from Corinth while he was in Macedonia (see 2 Cor. 2:12–13; 7:5–16). Paul then wrote the letter we know as 2 Corinthians.

Paul perhaps revealed more of himself in the Letter of 2 Corinthians than in any other epistle except Galatians. He intended in 2 Corinthians to defend his ministry and the integrity of the truth of Jesus Christ. He also explained beautifully the meaning of ministry in the name of Christ.

for proclamation. No need exists for faint-heartedness, concealment, or manipulation. As one serves in this ministry, he or she can have total boldness and confidence because the power to bring light to people comes not from the servant but from the Lord.

The "treasure" in verse 7 refers to the treasure of the "light of the knowledge of the glory of God in the face of Christ" (4:6). This treasure Paul held in "clay jars" (earthen vessels) to demonstrate that "the extraordinary power" that attends the preaching of the gospel stems from God, not from any human source. The "clay jars" probably referred to the cheap, fragile, easily broken, easily replaced pottery that could be purchased in the market place of Corinth.

Verses 8–11 convey Paul's concept of the apostolic ministry. The treasure is not diminished by the meager value of the container (4:8–9). Paul indicated that his constant experience was that of always being aware of his own limited capacity yet ever assured of God's continuing power to transform any and every situation that might seek to crush or immobilize him. From such faith and assurance flows the power for the ministry of reconciliation.

> *The power for the ministry of reconciliation rests not in the abilities or methods of people but only in the all-surpassing strength of God.*

The apostle indicated (4:10–11) that every day we experience something of the death of Christ so that through this suffering we might show the power of Jesus in our weak bodies. That Jesus might be seen in his glory is the purpose and consequence of our suffering. Death continues in the servant of Christ so that life may come in the experience of the ones served (4:10–11).

The power for the ministry of reconciliation rests not in the abilities or methods of people but only in the all-surpassing strength of God. We hold this ministry and the truth it contains in clay jars, which never detract from the glory of the message.

Assurance in the Ministry of Reconciliation (2 Cor. 4:12—5:10)

The apostle indicated the assurance that stimulates one to continue in the ministry of reconciliation. Faith in the Lord of the harvest allows one to

Paul's Establishing the Church at Corinth

Acts 18:1–18 tells of Paul's establishing the church at Corinth, probably in AD 50. There Paul served with Aquilla and Priscilla, believers who had fled from Rome.

Paul began his missionary work at Corinth in the synagogue. Jewish opposition led him to turn his ministry to the Gentiles, moving his service to the home of Titus Justus and in the company of Crispus, the ruler of the synagogue. Jewish leaders, who rejected the message of Jesus, continued to cause problems for Paul and the believers in Corinth. The Roman proconsul, Lucius Junius Gallio, who began his administration in Corinth in AD 51, refused to take up the Jewish case against Paul (Acts 18:12–17).

continue working in the Lord's fields. Believing in the Lord, the minister can continue in face of difficulties in the ministry, knowing that his or her sufferings will result in spiritual life for others (4:11–14). This assurance of godly fruit prevents God's servant from ever losing heart. Small and transitory troubles cannot compare with the glory of the enrichment in the fellowship that Christ achieves through them. The knowledge of the eternal glory assures the one engaged in the ministry of reconciliation (4:15–18).

> *Those who attempt the ministry of reconciliation must work from motives of selfless service.*

Assurance in the ministry of reconciliation rests on the believer's hope in the resurrection as well as in the believer's confidence in his or her acceptance before God, even at the judgment (5:1–10). The minister of reconciliation looks forward to the transitory being replaced by the eternal. This confidence leads the minister to one great aim—in life and in death to please the Lord (5:9–10).

Motivation for the Ministry of Reconciliation (5:11–21)

The ministry of reconciliation represents an awesome task that sometimes is filled with difficulties. Why then would one undertake such a calling? These verses answer this vital question.

A first motivation for the ministry of reconciliation is reverence toward God (5:11). The term "therefore" indicates that these words must be closely associated with the foregoing, that is, the teaching of the judgment seat of Christ at which the works of believers will be judged (5:10). "Fear" in 5:11 is the reverential awe believers feel toward their Lord whom they love and serve.

> *Sinful people can return to right relationship with God because of God's work in Christ.*

A second motivation for the ministry of reconciliation is selfless concern for others (5:11–13). Paul's reasons for defending his apostleship, his ministry, and his message rested not on any desire for personal vindication but rather on his desire that the Corinthians be able to answer those who troubled them (5:12). These troublemakers took pride in human positions and praise. Paul provided the Corinthians with replies to such people.

Some detractors had accused Paul of being out of his mind (5:13). So selfless was Paul's intent that he declared whether in or out of his mind it was for the Corinthians. Those who attempt the ministry of reconciliation must work from motives of selfless service.

A third motivation for the ministry of reconciliation is the certainty of the love of Christ for all people (5:14–15). The apostle probably referred to the love of Christ for all people as seen in Christ's atoning death for all who would believe (5:14–15). This "love" could, how-ever, mean Christ's love specifically for Paul. This love of Christ "urges" or "compels" (NIV) believers to ministry.

> *Every believer should accept and incorporate into his or her life this wonderful ministry of reconciliation that God has graciously given to all his followers.*

The motivation stemming from Christ's love finds its foundation in the reality of Christ's death for the salvation of all people. In Adam, all people are dead. In Christ, those who trust will be made alive. So great was the love of Christ for humankind that the purpose of his dying was that even while they still live, they should cease living for themselves. Rather they should live for him who died for them and rose again (5:15). One of the most tragic aspects of the Fall of Adam and Eve was introducing selfishness into humankind. This tendency to center on self cannot be overcome in fallen people by human effort or strength. Freeing believers from the bondage of sinful, selfish living was a reason for the sacrifice of Christ and must become a major reason for the Christian's service.

A fourth motivation for the ministry of reconciliation flows from the convictions concerning the advantages of one who is in Christ (5:16–19). One advantage of being in Christ is a new way of regarding others. Paul's conviction that Christ died for all and calls all believers into selfless service (5:15) freed Paul to accept a new and different viewpoint in regard to others (5:16).

> *In Christ, God makes sinful people right with himself.*

Since Paul's conversion, he no longer considered a person from an earthly view or in a merely human fashion. Paul even came to view Christ from the heavenly assessment rather than the human.

A second advantage to being "in Christ" is the radical change that can only be expressed as becoming a "new creation" (5:7). The believer becomes a new person altogether.

Everything pertaining to the process of making sinful people right with God, creating them to be new creations, and calling them to the ministry of reconciliation is "from God" (5:18). God was in Christ, making peace

The City of Corinth

In Paul's day, the city of Corinth constituted one of the foremost commercial cities in the Roman Empire. It was located on a narrow isthmus between the port of Cenchreae (see Romans 16:1) on the Aegean Sea and the port of Lechlaeum on the Corinthian Gulf, which led to the Adriatic Sea. Goods were transported across the land rather than taking the long and dangerous journey around the peninsula. At one period, the Corinthians constructed a shipway over which they could drag smaller vessels.

The population of Corinth represented a melting pot of peoples from over the Empire. Among this polyglot of peoples lived a sizeable group of Jewish people, including Aquilla and Priscilla, Christians who had been expelled from Rome by Emperor Claudius' decree (Acts 18:2–4).

Corinthians served two patron deities—Poseidon, god of the sea, and Aphrodite, goddess of sexual activity. The temple of Aphrodite boasted 1,000 female prostitutes available to citizens and visitors alike. The proceeds from this activity provided much of the city's income. So intense was the sinfulness of the city that the Greeks invented the word "to Corinthianize," which meant to live an immoral lifestyle. To call a woman a "Corinthian" was to charge her with indecent conduct.

---

between the world and himself. In Christ, God makes sinful people right with himself.

A fifth motivation for the ministry of reconciliation springs from the realization of the responsibility God places on believers (5:18–19). Paul taught that God "has given us the ministry of reconciliation" (5:18). God gave us the work of making peace.

In 5:19 Paul intensified this teaching. God saved us and forgave our sins (5:19). Then God entrusted "the message of reconciliation to us" (5:19). The clear idea is that God intended for the redeemed to accept the gracious privilege of proclaiming this wonderful message of reconciliation. Sinful people can return to right relationship with God because of God's work in Christ.

Verse 20 proclaims that believers have become "ambassadors for Christ." We are the Lord's envoys or special messengers. An ambassador acts and speaks not only on behalf of his or her Lord but also in place of the sovereign from whom he or she received the commission. This ambassador must faithfully and precisely communicate the message entrusted to him or her.

The plea to be reconciled to God is not some impersonal or dispassionate message. The messenger entreats the lost to accept Jesus' offer and be made right with God.

The basis for this ministry of reconciliation lies in the act of God that made Christ, who knew no sin, to become sin for us so that we might come into right relationship with God. Christ takes on our sin and produces in us his rightness. Here is the essence of the selfless service for Christ. We beg others to allow God's gift to become real in their lives so that they too can know peace with God.

Believers become the envoys or ambassadors of Christ to proclaim the power and willingness of God to make repentant people right with God and give them peace.

Every believer should accept and incorporate into his or her life this wonderful ministry of reconciliation that God has graciously given to all his followers.

Conclusion

Grace and grace alone brings eternal life. One who experiences this new life, however, will begin to share in the wonderful and gracious ministry of reconciliation. Such selfless ministry can only be realized after one comes to Christ. One then works, not from motives of human desires, but from the constraint of Christ's love. Believers become the envoys or ambassadors of Christ to proclaim the power and willingness of God to make repentant people right with God and give them peace. The new life in Christ allows sinful people to have their sin forgiven, become in right relationship with God, and find peace with others as well.

QUESTIONS

1. What fears or anxieties cause you to neglect your Christian ministry? What do Paul's statements in 2 Corinthians 4:7–10 say to these fears?

2. What evidences do you see in your life that you have become a new creation and are now living for others rather than for yourself?

3. Why do you think you are not more "compelled" by Christ's love to witness and serve others?

4. When do you feel most fervently the responsibility of being the representative of Christ to the lost and to other believers?

5. Describe the person or people you think most exemplify the characteristics of a selfless servant. What would need to change in your life to help you become more of a selfless servant?

Focal Text

Hebrews 11:1–2, 8–28; 11:32—12:3

Background

Hebrews 11:1—12:17

Main Idea

Having Christian faith means keeping on living faithfully to God, even when life is difficult.

Question to Explore

What is faith, anyway?

Study Aim

To measure my faith by the best models of faith in biblical history

Study and Action Emphases

- Equip people for ministry in the church and in the world

LESSON TEN

A Faith That Means Faithfulness

Quick Read

Faith, the God-given capacity to be certain that God exists and will keep his promises, enables believers to live faithfully and gives them strength in the face of all difficulties.

The story goes that two young boys walking home from Sunday School were discussing the morning's lesson. One asked, "Just what is faith anyhow?"

The second answered, "Well, faith is believing what you know ain't really true!" Surely there is a better answer.

The Epistle to the Hebrews teaches that faith enables us to be certain of the truth of God's message and be convinced of the reality of things that cannot be seen with human eyes. The book declares that faith is the "assurance" of the things we hope for and that faith convinces us that God's promises are certain and secure (Hebrews 11:1–2). Furthermore, faith guides believers to understand how they should live in view of these assurances. Faith goes beyond believing to doing. The absolute assurance of the reliability of God and the certainty of God's promises empowers believers to faithful living, even when life confronts them with difficult situations.

How can Christians continue to serve and live for God when troubles, persecutions, difficulties, and problems arise? The Epistle to the Hebrews answers by saying that if we believe God exists and are convinced that God will keep his promises we can continue to live faithfully.

The writer of Hebrews sought to encourage the letter's recipients, Jewish Christians, to remain true to Christ and resist all pulls toward failing to be faithful to the Christian faith. He made this plea by pointing to the superiority of Christ to everything in Jewish religion. Christ is a revelation superior to that of the prophets (Heb. 1:1–2) and the angels (1:4–14), a servant superior to Moses (3:1—4:13), an intermediary superior to the Jewish priesthood or Melchizedek (4:14—10:18), and a new and living way to God superior to all others (10:19–25). Because of this superiority of Christ, believers can and should draw near to God and hold fast to the essentials of the Christian faith (10:19–39). Christ's superiority motivates Christians to continue to live the Christian life faithfully and resist all efforts to draw them back to Jewish religion and lifestyle.

The writer illustrated his teaching by using the accounts of heroes of the faith who lived faithfully even in the face of difficulties and persecutions (11:1–40). The letter then calls for actions that indicate faith in light of these models provided by people of faith (12:1—13:25). The epistle promises us that faith enables Christian living by (1) assuring us of the truth of the Christian message, (2) empowering us for faithful conduct, and (3) comforting or strengthening us in the face of all trials.

Hebrews 11:1–2, 8–28; 11:32–40

[1]Now faith is the assurance of things hoped for, the conviction of things not seen. [2]Indeed, by faith our ancestors received approval. [3]By faith we understand that the worlds were prepared by the word of God, so that what is seen was made from things that are not visible.

. . . .

[8]By faith Abraham obeyed when he was called to set out for a place that he was to receive as an inheritance; and he set out, not knowing where he was going. [9]By faith he stayed for a time in the land he had been promised, as in a foreign land, living in tents, as did Isaac and Jacob, who were heirs with him of the same promise. [10]For he looked forward to the city that has foundations, whose architect and builder is God. [11]By faith he received power of procreation, even though he was too old—and Sarah herself was barren—because he considered him faithful who had promised. [12]Therefore from one person, and this one as good as dead, descendants were born, "as many as the stars of heaven and as the innumerable grains of sand by the seashore."

[13]All of these died in faith without having received the promises, but from a distance they saw and greeted them. They confessed that they were strangers and foreigners on the earth, [14]for people who speak in this way make it clear that they are seeking a homeland. [15]If they had been thinking of the land that they had left behind, they would have had opportunity to return. [16]But as it is, they desire a better country, that is, a heavenly one. Therefore God is not ashamed to be called their God; indeed, he has prepared a city for them.

[17]By faith Abraham, when put to the test, offered up Isaac. He who had received the promises was ready to offer up his only son, [18]of whom he had been told, "It is through Isaac that descendants shall be named for you." [19]He considered the fact that God is able even to raise someone from the dead—and figuratively speaking, he did receive him back. [20]By faith Isaac invoked blessings for the future on Jacob and Esau. [21]By faith Jacob, when dying, blessed each of the sons of Joseph, "bowing in worship over the top of his staff." [22]By faith Joseph, at the end of his life, made mention of the exodus of the Israelites and gave instructions about his burial.

[23]By faith Moses was hidden by his parents for three months after his birth, because they saw that the child was beautiful; and they were not afraid of the king's edict. [24]By faith Moses, when he was grown up, refused to be called a son of Pharaoh's daughter, [25]choosing rather to share ill-treatment with the people of God than to enjoy the fleeting pleasures of

sin. [26]He considered abuse suffered for the Christ to be greater wealth than the treasures of Egypt, for he was looking ahead to the reward. [27]By faith he left Egypt, unafraid of the king's anger; for he persevered as though he saw him who is invisible. [28]By faith he kept the Passover and the sprinkling of blood, so that the destroyer of the firstborn would not touch the firstborn of Israel.

....

[32]And what more should I say? For time would fail me to tell of Gideon, Barak, Samson, Jephthah, of David and Samuel and the prophets—[33]who through faith conquered kingdoms, administered justice, obtained promises, shut the mouths of lions, [34]quenched raging fire, escaped the edge of the sword, won strength out of weakness, became mighty in war, put foreign armies to flight. [35]Women received their dead by resurrection. Others were tortured, refusing to accept release, in order to obtain a better resurrection. [36]Others suffered mocking and flogging, and even chains and imprisonment. [37]They were stoned to death, they were sawn in two, they were killed by the sword; they went about in skins of sheep and goats, destitute, persecuted, tormented—[38]of whom the world was not worthy. They wandered in deserts and mountains, and in caves and holes in the ground.
  [39]Yet all these, though they were commended for their faith, did not receive what was promised, [40]since God had provided something better so that they would not, apart from us, be made perfect.

Hebrews 12:1–3

[1]Therefore, since we are surrounded by so great a cloud of witnesses, let us also lay aside every weight and the sin that clings so closely, and let us run with perseverance the race that is set before us, [2]looking to Jesus the pioneer and perfecter of our faith, who for the sake of the joy that was set before him endured the cross, disregarding its shame, and has taken his seat at the right hand of the throne of God.

Faith Assuring of God's Truth (11:1–7)

The Epistle to the Hebrews assures us of the truth of God's message and the reliability of his promises. On the basis of this confidence, the writer called for perseverance in Christian living (10:35–39). Hebrews openly affirms that "faith is being sure of what we hope for and certain of what we do not see" (11:1–2, NIV).

The word *faith* in these verses does not refer simply to the state of believing in God but rather to an active conviction that moves and molds the conduct and lifestyle of believers. This faith assures believers that God's promises of hope remain real and valid.

In Hebrews, an unbreakable bond joins faith and hope. In fact, this epistle presents faith and hope as virtually interchangeable. Faith provides the confident assurance of the reality of the things being hoped for, the promised blessings from God

The word translated "assurance" in verse 1 holds deep meaning. The word describes faith as that which gives substance or provides confidence in the things hoped for that are as yet unseen.

> *How can Christians continue to serve and live for God when troubles, persecutions, difficulties, and problems arise?*

A second possible meaning of "assurance" is related to the idea of a foundation. Faith is the foundation or basis on which our hope is raised or the beginning on which certainty rests. Both Augustine and Aquinas interpreted the word in this way. They saw faith as the essence, the beginning or first principle of the things hoped for.

A third possible understanding of the word is indicated by the fact that some ancient writings use the term to refer to a document that attests to or provides for evidence of ownership. Thus, faith can be seen as the guarantee of the heavenly realities, envisioning them as rightfully belonging to us and assuring that we will partake of them.

"Assurance," *confident* assurance, is the fourth and most satisfactory meaning of the word (see Heb. 3:14; 2 Corinthians 9:4; 11:17).

Thus, faith is not only the assurance of things we hope for although we have not yet seen them, but it also refers to the certainty or conviction of these unseen realities. Faith is the certainty of God's promises.

Faith, though, is not a static emotion. It is rather something lively and active that impels believers to reach out and grasp those realities on which hope is fixed.

Faith underlies the conviction that creation came into being at the will and act of God (Heb. 11:3). Furthermore, believers are pleasing to God on the basis of their faith in him. Abel, Enoch, and Noah pleased God because their faith in him allowed them to perform the actions for which they have become well known (11:4–7).

Verse 6 supplies a beautiful climax to this passage. The verse states that one cannot please God apart from faith. This is true because one who is

The Book of Hebrews

Hebrews likely was written between the time a little prior to AD 70, since it does not allude to the destruction of the temple in Jerusalem that occurred then, and prior to AD 95, when Clement of Rome wrote his letter to the Corinthians and showed acquaintance with Hebrews. An unknown Christian wrote this epistle to a group of Jewish Christians. They may have either lived in Rome or been acquainted with people in Rome (Hebrews 13:24). These Jewish Christians had faced persecution in the past. They were now showing signs of returning to Jewish religion, perhaps in an attempt to avoid further persecution (Heb. 6:4–8; 10:26–31; 12:14–17).

approaching God must believe not only that God exists, as important as that belief is, but also that God rewards those who diligently seek him. Faith believes that God exists and will keep his promises.

Faith Enabling for Life and Service (11:8–28)

This absolute conviction that God exists and will keep his promises enables believers to live faithfully in all circumstances. The author of Hebrews points to faith operating in the lives of various Old Testament people—Abraham, Isaac, Jacob, Joseph, Moses, and others—enabling these heroes of faith to follow God's will for proper living.

Faith enabled Abraham to leave Chaldea, a land at that time blessed with safety and prosperity, for an unknown inheritance in obedience to God's call (11:8). True faith leads to decisive action.

Faith is the certainty of God's promises.

Abraham left Chaldea for a promised inheritance he had not seen and a location he did not know. He lived in tents (11:9; suggesting that which is temporary) and looked forward to the city "that has foundations, whose architect and builder is God" (11:10).

Verse 11 describes how through faith Abraham and Sarah—"even though he was too old—and Sarah herself was barren" had a child. Through Abraham, though he was "as good as dead," there came descendants (11:12).

All the heroes of faith had died still looking for the final promise of God. Faith allowed them to view the yet unfulfilled promise as a present reality. God's promise was in their minds and hearts (12:13–14). These believers refused to think about any idea of returning to the lands they had left. Is this perhaps a veiled plea against returning to Jewish religion? They looked forward to the final promise of God. Because of this faith, God was not ashamed to call them his people and has prepared a city for them (11:15–16).

True faith leads to decisive action.

Verses 17–19 recalled Abraham's most severe trial. This trial required more trust and revealed more than any other the rocklike firmness of Abraham's faith. The severity of the trial involved offering the son of whom God himself had said, "It is through Isaac that descendants shall be named for you" (11:18; see Genesis 21:12). Abraham "considered" that God could even raise the dead, and he did at least figuratively receive Isaac back from the dead.

Verses 20–22 relate to Isaac's faith in blessing Jacob and Esau, Jacob's faith in blessing the sons of Joseph, and Joseph's faith in mentioning the coming exodus from Egypt. Faith enabled each patriarch to believe in the reality of the future of God's people.

In verse 23, the author turned to the example of another person of faith, Moses, whose parents hid him for three months (11:23). God enabled these parents to overcome fear and to defy the pharaoh through faith.

Verses 24–26 detail how Moses upon reaching maturity turned his back on the advantages of Egyptian society and joined in the difficulties of the sorely afflicted people of God. Moses considered abuse and suffering with God's people to be far more advantageous than all the wealth of Egypt. Again, the author emphasized accepting the way of obedience and suffering not by constraint,

The presence of "so great a cloud of witnesses" constitutes a valid reason for striving for the goal of faithful Christian living (12:1).

but willingly and joyfully, due to the conviction of the glory of the future reward.

Moses' journey from Egypt followed the promise of faith (11:27–28). Like his parents, Moses did not fear the anger of the pharaoh. Moses rather looked to God. "He persevered as though he saw him who is invisible" (11:27). Faith also enabled Moses so that he "kept the Passover and the sprinkling of blood" (11:28). Obviously, this obedient act pictures the death of Christ, the Lamb of God. Faith enabled Moses and the people to trust in the blood on the doorpost and the safety of their firstborn.

Faith enabled Moses and the people to leave Egypt and pass through the Red Sea, "as if it were dry land" (11:29). That this crossing was a miraculous event is attested by the tragedy that awaited the pursuing Egyptians. Faith enables Christians to attempt the impossible and accomplish it!

Faith Comforting and Strengthening in Trials (11:32—12:3)

The author had related the history of faith up to the period of entry into the Promised Land. He realized that he had recounted sufficient illustrations that faith was indeed "the assurance of things hoped for, the conviction of things not seen" (11:1). Saying, "And what more shall I say," indicates that more elaboration was not needed (11:28). He then gave a general summary of the triumphant faith of God's people in the face of every kind of cruel persecution and opposition.

> . . . Christians should rid themselves of all that lessens their service, especially sin that clings to and entangles them.

The list of names in verse 32 mentions a few of many who deserved to be mentioned. The general nature of the list is indicated by prophets as a separate category with no direct mention of names.

Verses 33–38 chronicle the acts of faith that grew out of the belief of these persons who believed that God exists and that he will reward those who seek him. Through faith, these "conquered kingdoms," that is, won victories over formidable enemies (11:33; the judges and David). They "administered justice" (11:34; Samuel; David). They "obtained promises" (11:33). They "shut the mouths of lions," which is probably a reference to the deliverance of Daniel in Persia (11:33; see Daniel 6:22). They "quenched the fury of the flames," which probably refers to the fires of persecution such as the three Hebrew youth faced in Nebuchadnezzar's furnace (Dan. 3:17). They "escaped the edge of the sword," perhaps referring to David or Elijah when they were in danger of death from enemies (Heb. 11:34). Faith made all of these experiences possible.

The epistle turns from deeds done by faith to characteristics of these servants of God who found victory through faith (11:34). They "won strength out of weakness," became "mighty in war," and "put foreign armies to flight" (11:34). All these actions stemmed not from any ability of the people but from their faith in God.

Five Directions for Avoiding Spiritual Burnout

1. Remember the examples of those who have lived in faith.
2. Rid yourself of everything and anything—especially entangling sin—that hinders you from living the Christian life and serving the Lord
3. Continue with determination, resolution, and perseverance the life to which God has called you.
4. Maintain the view of Christ and his example of selfless service for others in doing the will of God.
5. Accept God's help in remaining steadfastly faithful.

Verses 35–38 report some of the intense sufferings endured by these who lived by faith. These endured persecution and torture rather than seeking escape by renouncing their faith. Once again the writer of Hebrews pleaded for endurance.

The writer declared that these were "commended for their faith" (11:39). He was referring to the entire succession of men and women who had remained faithful to God in the centuries leading up to the coming of Christ. This phrase could mean they won renown by their faith or more likely, they by their faith won God's approval. Certainly the meaning is that the most severe trials and sufferings did not extinguish their faith. Their faithfulness in the face of these trials declared the genuineness of their faith.

> *Jesus is the source and goal of our faith; it is on him that faith depends from start to finish.*

These faithful men and women did not during their earthly pilgrimage experience the glorious fulfillment of God's promises, that is, the coming of Christ. They did see this fulfillment through the eyes of faith and trusted in this vision. They lived and died in faith.

These faithful people were by no means barred from the full enjoyment of God's promises. The Old Testament saints looked forward to the better plan in the Messiah. Thus, a continuity and unity exists between all believers (11:39–40).

The author now applied the lesson that stemmed from the examples of those whose faith had triumphed over every testing experience (12:1–3). "Therefore . . . let us," associates the injunctions of this section with the illustrations of the previous section (12:1). In his plea to the readers, the

Faith Enabling Believers

- Faith enables believers to comprehend the truth of God's message and rest on it.
- Faith enables believers to understand God's call and obey it.
- Faith enables believers to attempt the impossible and accomplish it.
- Faith enables believers to face every trial and temptation to turn from God's will and remain faithful.

author used the imagery of the athletic contest. The competitors were surrounded by the spectators, who urged them on and motivated them to reach the goal. The presence of "so great a cloud of witnesses" constitutes a valid reason for striving for the goal of faithful Christian living (12:1).

Hebrews 12:1–3 enjoins four actions. It encourages first, "let us also lay aside every weight and the sin that clings so closely" (12:1). The teaching is to strip off or throw aside anything that hinders from the full service of Christ. As the Greek athlete shunned all external matters that would encumber his performance, Christians should rid themselves of all that lessens their service, especially sin that clings to and entangles them.

The second encouragement is, "let us run with perseverance the race that is set before us" (12:1). These believers needed to regain their desire and continue with faithfulness in the race God had set for them. This race is to be run with "perseverance" (or determination, endurance, resolution).

The third encouragement is, "looking to Jesus" (12:2). Believers should be totally involved with Jesus and set their purposes on him.

Jesus is "the pioneer and perfecter of our faith" (12:2). By his action, he "endured the cross," He now "has taken his seat at the right hand of the throne of God" (12:3). Jesus is the source and goal of our faith; it is on him that faith depends from start to finish.

The actions of the Savior reached a zenith on the cross, where he took our place so he could give us his right standing with God. The motive for the cross was first for our salvation but also for the sake of "the joy that was set before him," that is, for the sake of the joy of completing the work of salvation that he had come to perform to the glory of the Father (12:2).

The fourth encouragement, "Consider him who endured . . . so that you may not grow weary or lose heart," summarizes the epistle's teaching (12:3). These Hebrew believers were tending to think of the allure of the world. They were considering turning back to the theology of the

Judaizers and giving up the struggle. This act would, they thought, relieve their sufferings. The writer stressed the need to take a close look at Christ, compare oneself to him, and take one's standard from him. Look at the life of Jesus, and from Jesus' sacrifice and commitment draw your direction.

Jesus' life showed steady endurance to the hostility directed against him by sinners. The final purpose of the readers' so considering Jesus and his atoning work is that they will "not grow weary or lose heart" (12:3). The suffering of Christ's followers is always light

> *Look at the life of Jesus, and from Jesus' sacrifice and commitment draw your direction.*

when compared to the sufferings of Christ. Here the encouragement to persevere reaches its most dramatic expression. The call is for faithful living in the face of any and every attempt by Satan to pull us aside.

Conclusion

Christians in every age are tempted to compromise and turn away from the path of living mapped out by the Lord. The emphasis of the Letter to the Hebrews remains as contemporary as tomorrow's headlines. Faith, which consists of believing in God's existence and his faithfulness in keeping his promises, enables believers to continue living faithfully in the face of all difficulties, sufferings, persecutions, and trials. As we keep our eyes on Christ and conform to his example and standards, we will continue to live and serve faithfully.

QUESTIONS

1. What makes you certain of the truth of the message of the Bible and of God's promises?

2. What tempts you to turn aside from the Christian life? Before you dismiss this question by simply saying, "Nothing could do that," think of these matters. Are you ever tempted to take a certain stand because you think that taking the biblical stand would cost you status, money, or ease? Do you ever base your decisions on what you think will be for your good rather than the truth of God?

3. Who are your primary "heroes," that is, the people to whom you look for inspiration and challenge in the Christian life?

4. How would you explain to an unbeliever why you try to live the Christian life even when it seems to cost you?

Focal Text

1 John 4:7–21

Background

1 John 4:7–21

Main Idea

Because God has loved us, we are to love one another, thus demonstrating the genuineness of our relationship to God.

Question to Explore

Do we really have to love *everybody*?

Study Aim

To decide on ways I will demonstrate my love for other people this week

Study Actions and Emphases

- Share the gospel of Jesus Christ with all people
- Minister to human needs in the name of Jesus Christ
- Equip people for ministry in the church and in the world
- Develop Christian families
- Strengthen existing churches and start new congregations

LESSON ELEVEN

Love, the Heart of the Gospel

Quick Read

This portion of 1 John focuses on ethical living. The passage shows the connection between love for others and the authenticity of one's Christian profession.

For several years, I taught high school biology and chemistry. Although on first glance these fields seem vastly distant from Christian ethics, the discipline I now teach at Hardin-Simmons University, there are great similarities.

Chemistry and biology work with functional, application points of life. Christian ethics is applying one's faith to everyday dimensions of life. Both chemistry and biology use methods for testing and quantifying observations. These disciplines call for laboratory experience. Similarly, Christian ethics offers ways to consider the authenticity of one's faith by its application to the issues of life. In fact, 1 John 4:7–21 is a primary resource for how Christians are to live in the laboratory of life.

First John is built around proofs or tests for determining the authenticity of one's profession of faith. These tests include: obedience to Christ (see 1 John 2:3–6; 2:28—3:10); love (see 2:7–11; 3:11–24; 4:7–21); and belief (see 2:18–27; 4:1–6).

John calls believers to apply the tests to their lives. In addition, he also invites true believers in Christ to find assurance of their relationship in God.

With 1 John 4, the order of the tests is rearranged from earlier presentations. Here the test of belief is in verses 1–6. The test of love comes with verses 7–11. Then a combination of love and belief comes in verses 12–21. Apparently, John had in mind with this structure to emphasize love in chapter 4.

Love Is from God (4:7–11)

In English only one word communicates the many meanings for love. The range can be seen, and felt, as one may say, *I love chocolate ice cream* or *I love my children*. The emotions are different. The meaning is different in its import.

The Greek language provided several words with which to say *love*. Each way gave a particular emphasis. *Philia* conveyed friendship love. Not accidentally, the Pennsylvania city, Philadelphia, finds it basic name in *philia* and is also known as the "city of brotherly love."

The Greek word *eros* described sexual love. However, "desire" is a major part of its meaning. Perhaps obviously to the reader, desire can have extraordinarily negative meanings as well as positive ones. Note how the English word *erotic* is rooted in the Greek term.

1 John 4:7–21

[7]Beloved, let us love one another, because love is from God; everyone who loves is born of God and knows God. [8]Whoever does not love does not know God, for God is love. [9]God's love was revealed among us in this way: God sent his only Son into the world so that we might live through him. [10]In this is love, not that we loved God but that he loved us and sent his Son to be the atoning sacrifice for our sins. [11]Beloved, since God loved us so much, we also ought to love one another. [12]No one has ever seen God; if we love one another, God lives in us, and his love is perfected in us.

[13]By this we know that we abide in him and he in us, because he has given us of his Spirit. [14]And we have seen and do testify that the Father has sent his Son as the Savior of the world. [15]God abides in those who confess that Jesus is the Son of God, and they abide in God. [16]So we have known and believe the love that God has for us.

God is love, and those who abide in love abide in God, and God abides in them. [17]Love has been perfected among us in this: that we may have boldness on the day of judgment, because as he is, so are we in this world. [18]There is no fear in love, but perfect love casts out fear; for fear has to do with punishment, and whoever fears has not reached perfection in love. [19]We love because he first loved us. [20]Those who say, "I love God," and hate their brothers or sisters, are liars; for those who do not love a brother or sister whom they have seen, cannot love God whom they have not seen. [21]The commandment we have from him is this: those who love God must love their brothers and sisters also.

These two terms for love were used a great deal in the larger society of the New Testament world. *Eros* is not used in the New Testament, however.

The Greek word for love appearing most in the New Testament is *agape*. *Agape* is self-giving love. The concept moves the individual to a loftier application of love than either of the former terms. Rather than being possessive, as *eros* suggests, or limited to those like us, as *philia* describes, *agape* is extended to those who do not merit affection, warmth, or care. In short, *agape* is the love flowing from God to people.

The main idea of this section is that *agape* is to be demonstrated especially between Christians. More than an implication, however, is that the true Christian also treats all fellow humans with this *agape*. The section begins and ends with the idea of "love one another." This was the imperative which Jesus gave the disciples in John 15:12–17.

The importance of the imperative form is that the disciples were left not to feelings but to choice and action. The basis for this love is found in the person and character of God. Thus, the source and dynamic for the love we extend to others is not only the energy *we* bring to bear to relationships; rather, the source of love is *God* (1 John 4:7).

One of the characteristics of this epistle is the stark contrasts; for example, life and death, light and darkness. In verse 8, one of these contrasts comes to the fore—love and hate. That is, one who does not love, or hates, another demonstrates that one is not related to God.

Introduction to 1 John

First John is part of the section of the New Testament called the General Letters. The General Letters were circulated among various Christian congregations of the first and second centuries rather than having been written to one location, such as Ephesus or Corinth.

The General Letters are usually short in length. First John may have been more of what in our day we call a tract or even a homily or sermon. With 1 John, no specific addressee is identified. No closing is given. No allusion is made to any location.

There is a strong sense, however, that the writer knew those who would receive the letter. Terms of endearment for the receivers of the material—such as "beloved" and "children"—depict a familiar relationship. Too, the collective "we" is used throughout the epistle. Thus, a joint understanding is implied.

One view is that 1 John was written in Ephesus. This city formed a kind of hub for information and commerce for its surrounding area. Thus, Asia Minor became the primary area of the letter's circulation.

First John addresses essentially one theme. The one theme finds several avenues of expression, however. Thus, although any believer can read the little book profitably, the book is theologically complex.

The one theme of the letter addressed a crisis of faith in the early church. This crisis stemmed from the spread of gnosticism. A mix of Eastern mysticism and Greek philosophy, gnosticism was close enough in some ways to Christianity that confusion ensued with Christian believers.

One of gnosticism's essential themes was that knowledge was the way to God. The Greek word *gnosis* lies at the root of the term gnosticism. Gnosticism's "knowing" God was an abstract knowledge.

First John maintains that knowing God is more than an abstract knowledge. Knowing God calls for relating to God. One knows God by information, content, data. More important, however, one knows God through a relationship that is reflected in how one relates to other people.

The strong contrasts of 1 John can be helpful. We sometimes know well the difficulty of moving emotionally and functionally from hate to love. For example, we know we need to love, but doing so is not easy. One suggestion is to think of the movement toward love as occurring in increments. One surely could admit that toleration is better than hate, that empathy is better than toleration, and that support and encouragement are better than empathy.

The closing clause of 4:8 is one of the most profound statements in the Bible. Here we learn that God is love. The essence of God's character and action is love.

God's love is the paradigm for how we are to show love.

Verses 9–11 elaborate on the statement, "God is love." God has approached humanity in the incarnation, sending his Son to give people the purpose in their lives that sin has damaged. God's love is the paradigm for how we are to show love. We are to initiate loving actions toward the unlovely.

The reader may sense a tone of obligation in John's language in 4:11. But the response of one who is loved is not necessarily duty. Rather, when we are loved, we find ourselves warmed, changed. We want to be channels to others of what we have experienced ourselves. We do not love because we have to, but because we want to.

Love Abiding in Us (4:12–16)

Verse 12 is a transitional verse between the ground of love and the actions of love. The ground of Christian love is that God is love. Even though one cannot see God, *agape* can be seen in action.

John's assertions and conclusions in verses 7–11 were quite enough to challenge the culture of his time. As do previous sections of 1 John, this section counters gnosticism, particularly with regard to love. John's call to love others moves the conversation from abstract concepts to people the readers knew, including themselves.

Christians must not only be able to describe love or even to know that God is love. They must live in the content and sphere of this love and thus actively engage it. The believer lives in God's presence, and God is with them and in them, abiding.

Abide, abides—these terms occur several times in these few verses (4:13, 15, 16). The usage is the same as found in John 15, where Jesus spoke of the disciples remaining in him, as vines or branches find their life's sustenance through the trunk.

The Apostle Paul's term "in Christ" supplies help for our understanding of *abide*. For Paul, there was a reciprocal relationship between the believer's being in Christ and Christ being in the believer. At three points in 1 John 4:13–21 (see 4:13, 15, 16) John offered evidence for this indwelling. The primary point of evidence is "because he has given us of his Spirit" (4:13). The statement can be understood both as having the presence of the Holy Spirit and expressing the character of the Holy Spirit.

> We are to initiate loving actions toward the unlovely.

But, we cannot see the Spirit of God. How can this be evidence? We gauge the evidence by recognizing the presence of the fruit of the Spirit (see Galatians 5:22–23).

Abiding is an important concept for our time. More than just a word, it contains content that can sustain us.

Every generation has demonstrated a need to have sacred space where God is worshipped. We see this need expressed in the Old Testament in the tabernacle and the temple.

At the same time, God's people are a sojourning people. We are in, but not, truly of this world, and we journey about in the world.

> The essence of God's character and action is love.

The dwelling and seeking images can be seen together in the exodus from Egypt. The people moved, they stopped, and they moved again. Ultimately, the nation found a stopping place.

Whether the people were stopped or moving, God was with them. God did abide with them wherever they were.

So with us. Whether we are stopped or moving, God abides with us. God provides a comfort to us, a help for our every need.

Love Perfected in Us (4:17–21)

Ripe, mature, whole, full, complete—all of these form the meaning of *perfected*. Perhaps it should go without saying, but none of the ways we understand or live out love in this life are perfect. The shape of that perfect love can begin to show, however.

Trinity

Although the word *trinity* is not a biblical term, the concept can be seen in the New Testament. *Trinity* does not refer to multiple gods. The Hebrews proclaimed they worshipped one God, and the New Testament continues this pattern.

In the New Testament, the Trinity can be identified through events such as Jesus' baptism (Matthew 3:13–17). As well, the Apostle Paul's salutations and benedictions indicate a three-fold description of God as Father, Son, and Holy Spirit. See, for instance, Romans 1:1–7.

Christians through the centuries have sought to understand and clarify the Trinity. Early Christian confessions of faith sought to do this, for example.

Modern Christians should give regular attention to understanding God as the Three-in-One. Such attention will consider the nature of God in creation, redemption, and judgment. As well, understanding the Trinity calls for giving attention to Jesus Christ's deity and incarnation. Perhaps ironically, the Holy Spirit calls for the most attention. Often this member of the Trinity is forgotten in Christian prayers. In addition, the Holy Spirit is the catalyst for demonstrating the ethical qualities of the Christian life.

This shape becomes more whole as one's abiding in God deepens. The deepening is a lifelong development, never reaching completion in this life.

John provides, again, some tests for recognizing this perfected love. First, perfected love provides boldness. Another word for boldness is *courage*. The word *courage* is not applied often enough to Christians. Expressing *agape* takes courage, however. Loving is sometimes difficult work.

Our thinking about courage may envision those notable types getting headlines for this

The ground of Christian love is that God is love.

or that daring act. There are lots of everyday heroes and heroines, however; their courage is equally admirable. Such people may not display outstanding acts of courageous love. Rather, they express their courage persistently and consistently as they live lives characterized by *agape* love.

Some of the most courageous and loving people I know, for example, are those who are single parents. They find ways to encourage and help their children, alone. Too, there are those, sometimes called the "sandwich generation," who care for their children and for their own parents.

Such examples show that *agape*, expressed with courage, is quantitatively different from just having a warm feeling and kindly attitude. Rather, *agape* means actually engaging in loving acts for other people.

Case Study

A young man in his middle twenties asks for some time to talk about his life. He wonders whether he is a Christian. He can relate a profession of faith and participation in church life. He also, however, has had some experiences that could be described as un-Christian. How would you counsel him from 1 John 4:7–21?

This boldness that 1 John highlights "casts out fear" (4:18), another test of the kind of love we have. What would your life be like without fear? Some people's lives could be described by describing their fears. I have related to students, for example, "Tell me something about your fears, and I will tell you something about your theology."

> Whether we are stopped or moving, God abides with us.

Think, though, what life would be like to live it fearlessly. Indeed, according to John, one benefit is to approach God's judgment of our lives without fear. More immediate in impact, though, is the benefit of living life, now, without fear. Where fear paralyzes or anxiety brings tenseness, love moves to lubricate relationships. Where fear can move to violence, love transforms potential violence into calm.

A further test of love is that of loving those who have kindred hearts in God. How do we relate to those we call Christian brothers and sisters? The relationships we have with them can be a source both for conflict and for growing in *agape*.

We carry a wrong assumption if we think loving is always easier and smoother among Christians. Church conflict is everywhere. Sometimes congregations are the most secular contexts of any in which we live life. One does not have to wonder long why some people are

> How do we relate to those we call Christian brothers and sisters?

not attracted to some churches. Such congregations profess they love one another but are always fighting. Thus, these places become occasions of testing the love we profess. Another way to say this is, *If you can be a Christian in a church, you can be a Christian anywhere!*

Such tests of love can serve as the basis for growing in love. The trials and strains of relationships are like the tension of physical exercise on muscles. Such exercise helps us toward growth in physical health, although we may not think that at the time we are exercising.

Agape love finds its primary application among those in Christian fellowship. Such love, however, cannot be limited only to that circle. In fact, if love is practiced only within a congregation, then we do well to ask, "Is this really *agape* love?"

What would your life be like without fear?

Reflection

Reread 1 John 4:7–21 now. Let it inform you as you look about you. Think about people who may be studying this passage with you, people who worship with you, people in your family, and people in the community you see occasionally. How does this passage speak to you about making those relationships better?

QUESTIONS

1. How would you communicate this thought to someone who is not part of your congregation? *Authentic Christians love other people in the way God loves them.*

2. What example can you provide of how you have moved from hate, to toleration, to empathy, and then to support for another person?

3. Read Galatians 5:22–23. Which of these qualities have you seen demonstrated in the lives of people you know? How were the "fruit of the Spirit" exhibited? How did you feel when you saw these qualities demonstrated?

4. What connection do you see between love and courage? What are some examples of love in action that required courage?

5. What are some strategies for helping your congregation, your group, or your family to become more loving?

Focal Text

2 Peter 3:3–15*a*

Background

2 Peter 3:3–15*a*

Main Idea

Because Christ's promised return is certain, we should live in faithfulness to him.

Question to Explore

When Jesus returns, will he find you faithful?

Study Aim

To identify reasons for believing in Christ's return and determine to be found faithful when he does

Study and Action Emphases

- Share the gospel of Jesus Christ with all people
- Equip people for ministry in the church and in the world

LESSON TWELVE   The Promise of His Coming

Quick Read

The second coming of Jesus Christ is a pronounced theme of the New Testament. The emphasis of the theme is on providing encouragement and calling us to faithfulness to Christ in daily living.

My church rearing did not endear me to consider matters surrounding the second coming of Jesus. Much speculation about the subject was done, based on weak biblical interpretation, for instance. Furthermore, little attention was given to what the ideas might mean for the here and now.

As we study this passage about the second coming, let us seek to discover how it applies to us now. Watch for ideas that lead to maturity of faith expressed in life, not just to speculation.

This passage focuses on one of the most distinctive points of the entire Bible regarding last things. Themes developed in other portions of the New Testament are brought together here in a creatively helpful way.

2 Peter 3:3–15a

3First of all you must understand this, that in the last days scoffers will come, scoffing and indulging their own lusts 4and saying, "Where is the promise of his coming? For ever since our ancestors died, all things continue as they were from the beginning of creation!" 5They deliberately ignore this fact, that by the word of God heavens existed long ago and an earth was formed out of water and by means of water, 6through which the world of that time was deluged with water and perished. 7But by the same word the present heavens and earth have been reserved for fire, being kept until the day of judgment and destruction of the godless.

8But do not ignore this one fact, beloved, that with the Lord one day is like a thousand years, and a thousand years are like one day. 9The Lord is not slow about his promise, as some think of slowness, but is patient with you, not wanting any to perish, but all to come to repentance. 10But the day of the Lord will come like a thief, and then the heavens will pass away with a loud noise, and the elements will be dissolved with fire, and the earth and everything that is done on it will be disclosed.

11Since all these things are to be dissolved in this way, what sort of persons ought you to be in leading lives of holiness and godliness, 12waiting for and hastening the coming of the day of God, because of which the heavens will be set ablaze and dissolved, and the elements will melt with fire? 13But, in accordance with his promise, we wait for new heavens and a new earth, where righteousness is at home.

14Therefore, beloved, while you are waiting for these things, strive to be found by him at peace, without spot or blemish; 15and regard the patience of our Lord as salvation.

Is the Lord Coming? (3:3–7)

Peter called the critics of Christianity "scoffers" (2 Peter 3:3). They approached life in a know-it-all, contemptuous way and mocked other people's perspectives.

The mocking style should not be found among Christians. Rather Christians should live their faith through the kinds of expressions found in 2 Peter 1:5–8. Whether by jeering words or body language, "mockers" demonstrate their lack of humility and caring relational skills.

In short, the scoffers' version of God was too small.

The scoffers to whom Peter referred asked (3:4), "'Where is the promise of his coming?'"

The Greek word used for "coming" in this verse is *parousia*. It means the *presence, coming,* or *arrival* of someone. Another word associated with the same concept is *apocalypse*, which means *the revealing* or *the revelation*, as in the New Testament book, Revelation.

The name for the kind of biblical literature that deals with the end times is apocalyptic literature. Second Peter 3 decidedly falls within this

Introduction to 2 Peter

The language in 2 Peter is rougher, less fluid than that of 1 Peter. One explanation is that Peter himself took the pen and wrote 2 Peter, while the Epistle of 1 Peter was penned by Silvanus, who had a better command of Greek style (1 Peter 5:12).

The early church was slow in including 2 Peter in the New Testament canon. Notice of 2 Peter appears first in a reference from Origen, a Christian leader in the third century AD.

Still, the book was canonized by the fourth century.

The book was written for general distribution. Thus, it is one of the General Letters. The primary reading audience could have been those who found themselves dispersed far from Jerusalem and other Christian population centers. A letter like 2 Peter would serve to inform and encourage.

Second Peter begins with the theme of the source of true knowledge. Chapter 2 considers false knowledge, particularly how to deal with false teachers. The third chapter, the primary passage for this lesson, deals with a special problem— discouragement among Christians. Thus 2 Peter 3 offers a response to discouragement by laying the foundation for hope.

category. Apocalyptic literature is found in the Old Testament, especially in the Book of Daniel. Some of the books of the Apocrypha, written between the time of the Old Testament and the New Testament, are apocalyptic in nature. In the New Testament, the Book of Revelation is the fullest New Testament expression of apocalyptic literature.

The theme of the second coming was deeply ingrained in early Christianity. Much time had passed since Jesus' ascension, described in Acts 1. Impatience for the second coming could have spawned scoffing, even by Christians. Moreover, the scoffing could have come from those who were not Christians and who wanted to undermine the Christian movement.

> *The second coming teaches about God's patience, trustworthiness, and faithfulness.*

The scoffers argued that disciples had come and gone and nothing had happened of significance. Things were the same as they had been since creation. The implication was that Christians were worshiping a God who was not big enough to get a second coming done.

The scoffing attitude can be expected. Now, for two thousand years, Christians have said, *Jesus is coming again.* For two thousand years, Christians have been asked to carry an attitude of expectancy. To this point, however, no return has happened as proclaimed in Acts 1.

The scoffing can affect well-intentioned Christians. Some attempt to put together schedules of Jesus' return as a way of responding to the scoffers. Some Christians find the ridicule something too difficult with which to deal. They retreat into disappointment or otherwise ignore the idea.

Millennial Views

Discussion of millennial views deals with the relationship of Christ's second coming and the 1,000-year period to which John referred in Revelation 20:4–6. This 1,000-year period relates to the reign of Christ over the earth.

Three views or interpretations of this reign are primary. Amillennialism does not consider an earthly reign of Christ between return and final judgment. The 1,000 years is considered symbolic. Postmillennialism is the view that the reign of God will be completed progressively on earth. Evil will cease, and peace will arrive. Premillennialism expects that Christ will return at the beginning of the millennium and that believers will be resurrected then. The resurrected ones will then reign for 1,000 years with Christ. These three views are the source of considerable debate, and there are many variations of these basic views.

Peter, though, gave solid advice about the second coming. His teachings indicate not only how to deal with the scoffing but also and primarily with how to consider the second coming.

Peter took the scoffers' remark about creation and built upon it. Peter first stretched the time line beyond the scoffers' sense of when the creation was. For the scoffers, the creation evidently was self-existent. For Peter, God had spoken it into existence (3:5). Then judgment came by means of a deluge of water.

So, scoffing at the second coming meant scoffing at the God who had created the world and sent judgment in the past. As judgment had occurred in that earlier time by means of water, so judgment by means of fire would come in the future

The Day of the Lord (3:8–10)

In these verses, Peter established that God's sense of timing with regard to the return of Jesus Christ was not as the same as that of humans. Drawing from Psalm 90:4, Peter put God's relationship to time into perspective. The interpretation is not that 1,000 years exactly equals one "God-day." Rather, the expanse of creation, the magnitude of God's personality, and the encompassing nature of salvation are such that humans can perceive only a small portion of these dynamics and themes.

Peter intended for his audience to see that repentance and redemption were more important than identifying the day and time of Christ's return.

Where we think in terms of *chronos* (clock time, calendar time), God works on a scale beyond time. Furthermore, God is not a mere extension of creation. Rather, God manages creation. Moreover, the how and when of all that exists and occurs in heaven and earth is managed by God.

In short, the scoffers' version of God was too small. Their perspective was based on a scale that was too tiny. Perhaps even Christians' scale of things can be too small.

Furthermore, the delay of the second coming can be seen as a worthy teaching tool. The second coming teaches about God's patience, trustworthiness, and faithfulness. "The Lord is not slow about his promise" (3:9).

Moreover, the grace of God is exhibited for as long as the second coming is delayed (3:9). The seeming delay gives time for repentance to happen. This repentance was to be more than mere sorrow. There was to be a turnaround of life. In 2 Peter, repentance is synonymous with conversion. This repentance carries a hope that endures, holding the believer through difficult times—even as one waits for the second coming.

Peter intended for his audience to see that repentance and redemption were more important than identifying the day and time of Christ's return. Repentance placed one in such a relationship with God that, for the believer, the time of the second coming becomes secondary.

> . . . God's grace toward the repentant and God's judgment on sin are certain and can be counted on to happen in a deliberate way.

Keeping biblical themes in proportion to one another is important. Peter reminded his readers, including us, that the second coming, like the flood, carries judgment for the lack of repentance. Which is more important, then, speculating about when Jesus is coming again or living life from the perspective of repentance?

Though the redemptive nature of God overrides the emphasis of judgment in God's character, judgment is still part of God's nature and character. Thus Peter mentioned an ancient term with which his audience would have been familiar, "the Day of the Lord" (3:10).

"The Day of the Lord" is a phrase found particularly in the Old Testament prophets (see Amos 5:18, 20). The usage continued through the 400-year intertestamental period separating the Old and New Testaments. The term applies to the last times.

> . . . Christians can have peace about the fact that God is in control of the affairs of creation.

The first portion of 3:10 associates the "day of the Lord" with how it will arrive—"like a thief." The phrase finds resonance in Matthew 24:36. The key word is "like" (2 Peter 3:10). The arrival will be unexpected, and things will not be the same after as before. The actions of a thief strike one unawares; people are caught off-guard. The advice is to be aware and to take pre-emptive action.

Peter developed his theme of judgment by fire further after having raised it in 5:7. The details have led some Christians to interpret that judgment will be by a nuclear war. Or perhaps the sun will go out of control or the earth will collide with another body in space. Speculating about the source of this fire or what this "fire" will be like is pointless, however.

Note that there are no allusions to date or time in these verses, either. Verse 10 leaves the timing up to God. Scoffers will come and go with the generations and centuries. However, God's grace toward the repentant and God's judgment on sin are certain and can be counted on to happen in a deliberate way. This arrangement should prompt believers to be watchful and to reflect on how they project the gospel to those about them.

What Sort of People Ought You to Be? (3:11–15*a*)

In 3:3–15*a*, Peter addressed at least two challenges to the early believers' faith. His earlier remarks in the chapter were directed toward how to deal with the scoffers. We can consider the scoffers to be an external challenge to Christians, external at least to their lives. Where the scoffers ridiculed the Christians, there could be encouragement and hope. No matter the crises, Christians can have peace about the fact that God is in control of the affairs of creation.

> *We are to live with a sense of abundant life now, but with the knowledge that God has even more in store for us.*

The Christians to whom Peter wrote also faced an internal challenge. This internal challenge was about their lifestyle. This challenge moves the Christian's attention from "out there" to "in here." Do you see how the certainty regarding the coming of Christ could lend to a lack of concern about the Christian life, even being lazy about it?

Thus, Peter moved the conversation to a more personal level. With his word "since" in 3:11, he established the groundwork. Then he in effect said, *Jesus' second coming is definite. In light of that inevitable end to reality as we know it, how will you live? Certainly you can confront and confound your detractors. But are you a better Christian for how you deal with these matters?*

Peter did not raise the questions and leave readers without further information. He followed with two statements (3:11–13; 3:14–15*a*) regarding the standards for a Christian lifestyle. He focused the believers' thinking on the kind of life one should live as one comes to understand the realities of the second coming.

First, believers are to live lives marked by holiness and godliness (3:11). Both terms point to the nature and character of God. The terms convey the expectation that believers are to reflect God's nature and character in daily life.

Apocalyptic References

The themes and images portrayed in 2 Peter 3 can be found in other books of the Bible and other books of that time. References can be found in such Bible passages as the following: Daniel; Matthew 24—25; Mark 13; Luke 17:26–35; 21:34–36; 1 Thessalonians 4:13–18; Revelation.

Holiness has an Old Testament background. Holiness means that people related to God are to be separate and apart from whatever detracts from their obedience, reverence, and love for God. This relationship is not only between the individual and God. The vertical relationship is authenticated in one's relationships with fellow human beings.

Other characteristics that are to mark believers' lives are patience and an earnest desire for Jesus' return (3:12). We are to live with a sense of abundant life now, but with the knowledge that God has even more in store for us.

Those who live with the values and attitudes of holiness, godliness, and patience will fit in the context of the kind of life that will follow the second coming. They will be quite comfortable and familiar with "new heavens and a new earth, where righteousness is at home" (3:13). Even the way Peter stated this image should sharpen the believer's sensitivity toward and desire for righteousness. Righteousness refers to right standing with God that results in fulfillment of living in the perfection of God's character.

Further, with his term "therefore" in 3:14, Peter was saying, in effect, *Based on these ideas,* "*be found by him at peace.*" The term for *peace* in the Old Testament is *shalom.* The term encompassed all the virtues, values, and attitudes that could represent the presence and reign of God. Such peace was to mark the life of believers as they looked toward Jesus' return.

QUESTIONS

1. How has your growth in maturity in faith been related to crises in your life?

2. Do you agree or disagree with the following statement? Why or why not? *Speculating on the date and time of Jesus' return can draw Christians away from the need for repentance in their daily lives and for extending the promises of the gospel to others.*

3. How can the discussion of the end times in this passage in 2 Peter bring a sense of comfort and encouragement to us?

Focal Text

Revelation 5

Background

Revelation 4—5

Main Idea

Because Christ has purchased our salvation and is thus the only one worthy of the highest praise of heaven and earth, let us worship him with all our being!

Question to Explore

Who deserves your highest praise?

Study Aim

To commit or re-commit myself to worship and serve Christ

Study Actions and Emphases

- Share the gospel of Jesus Christ with all people
- Equip people for ministry in the church and in the world

LESSON THIRTEEN

Worthy Is the Lamb

Quick Read

We can underestimate the Book of Revelation if we consider it only as that part of the New Testament that talks about the future. It forms one of the best guides for worship in the New Testament. This lesson emphasizes that Christ, the Lamb of God, is worthy of our highest praise and thus climaxes this quarter's study of the New Testament.

"What is the primary responsibility of the church," the teacher asked. A pause settled over the class. Then people began to raise their hands.

One student said, "Education."

Another said, "Fellowship."

A third said, "Outreach."

The teacher responded, "All those are good answers, but the umbrella that covers all these ideas is worship. Everything the church does needs to grow from worship. If worship of God through Jesus Christ in the power of the Holy Spirit is not primary, where will the motivation come for education, fellowship, or outreach?"

This lesson's study can deteriorate into only a conversation about the oddities of the Book of Revelation. Read and study this passage, though, with a sense of wanting to learn more about worship and put it into practice.

About the Book of Revelation

The Revelation of John likely is the most difficult New Testament book for contemporary Christians to read, interpret, and apply. This difficulty is, no doubt, because of the strangeness of the material. The symbolic nature of the Revelation is foreign to contemporary Christians.

Too often, the book gets ignored. Ignoring the book may occur literally as readers move on to other New Testament materials. Another kind of ignoring comes from those whom I call the biblical speculators. These are those who treat the book as if it were a secret code to all manner of things. Typically their interpretations lack further scriptural grounding.

History teaches us that interpreters who identify specific symbols with specific events in their generation will miss the mark. Consistently, predictions revolving around certain symbols or themes fall flat. The predictors may even revise their dates, places, and personalities. Too easily, this practice falls into hucksterism, prostituting the Word of God for filthy lucre's sake.

Any of us will make a mistake if we attempt to reduce Revelation to having application only to our time. There is a pretentiousness with this kind of interpretation unbecoming to a Christian. One who engages in a serious study of Revelation will learn quickly that the book's themes push back the walls of our understanding of God, the kingdom of God, the redemptive work of Jesus Christ, and the continuing work of the Holy Spirit on a scale beyond our widest, deepest, broadest imaginations.

Revelation 5

[1]Then I saw in the right hand of the one seated on the throne a scroll written on the inside and on the back, sealed with seven seals; [2]and I saw a mighty angel proclaiming with a loud voice, "Who is worthy to open the scroll and break its seals?" [3]And no one in heaven or on earth or under the earth was able to open the scroll or to look into it. [4]And I began to weep bitterly because no one was found worthy to open the scroll or to look into it. [5]Then one of the elders said to me, "Do not weep. See, the Lion of the tribe of Judah, the Root of David, has conquered, so that he can open the scroll and its seven seals."

[6]Then I saw between the throne and the four living creatures and among the elders a Lamb standing as if it had been slaughtered, having seven horns and seven eyes, which are the seven spirits of God sent out into all the earth. [7]He went and took the scroll from the right hand of the one who was seated on the throne. [8]When he had taken the scroll, the four living creatures and the twenty-four elders fell before the Lamb, each holding a harp and golden bowls full of incense, which are the prayers of the saints. [9]They sing a new song:

> "You are worthy to take the scroll
> and to open its seals,
> for you were slaughtered and by your blood you ransomed for God
> saints from every tribe and language and people and nation;
> [10]you have made them to be a kingdom and priests serving our God,
> and they will reign on earth."

[11]Then I looked, and I heard the voice of many angels surrounding the throne and the living creatures and the elders; they numbered myriads of myriads and thousands of thousands, [12]singing with full voice,

> "Worthy is the Lamb that was slaughtered
> to receive power and wealth and wisdom and might
> and honor and glory and blessing!"

[13]Then I heard every creature in heaven and on earth and under the earth and in the sea, and all that is in them, singing,

> "To the one seated on the throne and to the Lamb
> be blessing and honor and glory and might
> forever and ever!"

[14]And the four living creatures said, "Amen!" And the elders fell down and worshiped.

A New Testament professor many years ago gave these suggestions for understanding the import of this New Testament book:

1. Remember, the main point of the book is in 1:1: "The revelation of Jesus Christ."
2. Read the book through as quickly as you can, but with an understanding of the flow of information.
3. Find someone about ten to twelve years old and explain to that person what you have read.

With this approach, the professor explained, one will grasp the major themes of the book but not get overwhelmed with details. The primary

The Book of Revelation

The Book of Revelation was written in the late first century. It appears to have been written for the sake of early Christians who were suffering untold persecution for their faith.

John put those first readers' perspective on this persecution into a broader understanding. For one thing, they needed to know that persecution for their faith was not unusual but rather was to be expected. As well, they needed to know that relative to the scale of the kingdom of God, their persecution was a rather small part of it. Finally, Revelation demonstrates that the Suffering Church was going to be ultimately a Victorious Church. Sin, Satan, and evil would have their day, but, in the last analysis, God was going to be victorious. Such a thought can be fortifying and encouraging to one for whom life has turned ugly.

John communicated these marvelous, expansive themes largely through what is called Jewish apocalypticism. The terminology can be traced back through the intertestamental period and into especially the times of bondage undergone by the Jews in the last several hundred years before Christ. During that time frame, much of it marked by persecution, the Jewish theologians developed frameworks to describe and interpret the times for their audiences. They strove to help their readers and hearers to keep the present difficulties in perspective. They emphasized that God was still with them.

The style of communication used in apocalyptic literature is marked by large themes—good and evil; light and darkness; creation and destruction; loss and salvation; history and future. This apocalypticism carried forward into and past the era of John.

John's first readers would have been familiar with the use of the highly symbolic language of apocalyptic literature. Their persecutors would not have understood.

theme, as is true of the New Testament as a whole, is that of putting forward the message of the gospel of Jesus Christ. We must beware of losing this important emphasis.

The retelling of one's reading of Revelation, suggested the professor, becomes an application of the material. One could assert that we have not really learned anything until we can tell someone else about it. Even as we tell what we have read, we will learn more as we consider how to put the ideas into words.

A Book of Great Worth (5:1-5)

Some of the significance of these verses can be lost on us. You may be surprised by this thought, but most who read these lines are among the most literate people of the world, of any time. Books and reading are simply part of what we do all the time. Whether it is something from the best-seller lists, the daily newspaper, or text on a computer screen, we are accustomed to words being available to us.

One who engages in a serious study of Revelation will learn quickly that the book's themes push back the walls of our understanding of God, the kingdom of God, the redemptive work of Jesus Christ, and the continuing work of the Holy Spirit on a scale beyond our widest, deepest, broadest imaginations.

Printing multiple copies of a book was unheard of in John's day. The invention of the printing press was one of those phenomenal developments that changed history. The printed word and reading became more and more accessible to more and more people. Still, printing came relatively late historically.

To the time of Gutenberg's printing press, books—anything to be read—was written by hand. Copies were made by hand and were rare. Most populations were illiterate.

Perhaps we should from time to time be aware of how our days and lives would be different without printed words. For some of us, indeed, fewer words would be an easier life. Imagine life, though, if all your newspapers, books, computers, copiers, and so forth were gone. We would be rather destitute intellectually and emotionally. We would likely notice a shriveling of our spirit, as well.

Therefore, this scroll—the book of that day—held up for those around the throne to see, takes on immense importance, simply because it is a book or scroll. What the scroll says is not given. We can surmise that the scroll is the Word of Life or Book of Life. Because of the ultimate significance of the scroll, the audience about the throne was overwhelmed by it.

Where is the place of the Book, the Word of God, for us? Is it a decoration? Do we understand it to hold the words of life?

> *The intent of this passage was for John's original audience to be moved to a sense of worship. The contemporary reading of the passage should bring no less a response.*

Several years ago a teacher of university students drew near to his death. He asked one nearby to bring him "the Book."

The young friend responded, "Do you mean the Bible?"

The dying man said, "When one is dying, the only book he or she wants is the Bible."

The emotion of John's experience increased as a plea was issued for someone to open the scroll. At first, there was "no one" (5:3). The effect of this on John was immense. The impact was this: the scroll held the keys to life in its abundance and its ultimate fulfillment. But, there was apparently and immediately none who could unlock its power.

This theme appears throughout literature—the power to resist and overcome evil is locked away and only a hero can save the day, the town, and the world. Without the hero and the power to overcome, all is lost.

This theme finds its ultimate height in Revelation 5. The search for meaning leads to a scroll to be opened, but no one can open it. The search for a hero, at first, turns up empty-handed.

Yet, John's account moves quickly. One of the characters around the throne identified a hero, a Savior—the "Lion of the tribe of Judah, the Root of David" (5:5). The identifying terms are familiar to one who understands the lineage of Jesus Christ. As well, an expectation had run through Jewish theology for centuries that the Messiah would be a military hero. This hero would throw off the shackles of whatever despot controlled the Jews. Whoever could break the seals on the scroll would have to be stronger and carry more authority than any ruling power in the world. A hero had been found!

A Lamb? (5:6–8)

John looked at the spot where he expected to see the Lion of Judah. Yet, in one of the most striking changes of images in the Bible, when they

Theology and Literary Forms in Revelation

The Book of Revelation did not exist in a world of its own, apart from the rest of the New Testament canon. The book was considered canonical relatively early. The authoritativeness related, as much as anything, to the basic apostolic theology running through the core of the book. This theology reflected the saving acts of God through the death and resurrection of Jesus. That same Jesus reigned with God. Those who confess the person of Jesus Christ as Lord of life will experience redemption. The Holy Spirit is poured out on those who name Christ as Lord. Those who are related to Christ will participate in a fellowship of worship and education. The same Christ will come again.

The book comes with as much diversity of form as any in the New Testament. Visions, symbols, prophecy, homilies, Scripture references, narrative, prayer, dialogue, and hymns all find place in expressing the basic theology. The book is a model for the variety of expressions Christians can use toward worship of God.

---

looked they did not see a Lion. Rather, they saw a Lamb. This Lamb stood ready to break the seals of the scroll.

The image of the Lamb takes more than a first, quick glance, as well. The Lamb was "as if it had been slaughtered" (5:6). Your mind's picture of a slaughtered lamb likely would not fit this picture that begins to unfold from John's pen, however.

Where we would expect a lamb lying across an altar or in some such position, this one was standing. The slaughtered Lamb was *alive.* Then, an image comes that we might expect from an artist such as Dali. This Lamb had not merely two each of horns and eyes; it had seven of each! Indeed, this was no ordinary Lamb.

> *Is it too much to conceive that the creation is already proclaiming the glory and praise of God? Are we too entangled in the things of life to realize it?*

This unusual Lamb moved unhesitatingly to take the scroll. Only one familiar to the one sitting on the throne knew the scroll and how to take it, or was allowed to have it. This Lamb can be seen throughout the rest of the Book of Revelation. Beginning in Revelation 6, the Lamb opened the seals locking the scroll. This Lamb was the one sought and the one needed to break the power of evil and provide redemption.

How do we understand this unfolding picture? Since the book is the Revelation of Jesus Christ, that is the place to begin.

151

The reader would not be far off the mark to understand that Jesus had been expected (as the Lion) to ride a warhorse and throw off Roman rule. The Messiah, instead, had responded with a different way to bring the kingdom of God to this world. Like a lamb led to the slaughter, Jesus had submitted to his crucifixion. This cruelly imposed death was intended to break the influence of the one who claimed to be the Messiah. Instead, he overcame death and the grave to be resurrected, something which each of his followers will experience. The seven horns depicted complete, ultimate power in the ancient world. The seven eyes describe the ability to be everywhere.

What we can draw from John's experience on Patmos as he observed what he described in Revelation 5 is that worship can happen anywhere and anytime for us.

Thus, these paradoxical images portray God the Father on the throne, the mission and ministry of Jesus Christ, and the work of the Comforter. These few verses—5:6–8—provide a synopsis of the gospel.

The Lamb, Worthy of Worship (5:9–14)

By now, in chapter 5, quite a lot has happened around the throne. The reader who does not want to get lost in details could stop reading at the end of verse 8. Certainly, however, I am not suggesting that be done. Yet, the essentials of the gospel have been related by John. The key figure, Jesus Christ, has begun to address alienation from God and make redemption available to the world.

Chapter 5 continues to move to a crescendo, however. As in the end of chapter 4, there is worship. As chapter 5 builds, there comes the realization

Activities to Enhance Your Study

- Find a recording of Handel's *Messiah* and play the chorus, "Worthy Is the Lamb That Was Slain." The text of this chorus comes from Revelation 5:12–13. Or find a printed copy of *The Messiah* and read this same chorus aloud.
- Scan a hymnal. Find hymn texts that contain apocalyptic references.
- Do the exercise suggested by the New Testament professor under the heading, "About the Book of Revelation."

of the grandeur of what is happening. Worship brings the scene in Revelation 5 to a climax. Consider both of these chapters together, and you will see the grand vision expand from God to Christ to the living creatures, to the twenty-four elders, to an unnumbered host, until everything everywhere worships God as Creator and Redeemer.

One mark that one has truly worshipped is that something about God and the kingdom is more plain to us.

Think about the persecuted Christians in John's era as they read Revelation. When they finished Revelation 5, they had a solid foundation for understanding that their destinies were secure with God. No power on this earth or beyond was supreme to the Lamb.

Those about the throne recognized the significance of what they had witnessed. Before their eyes had been acted out the process of redemption involving God the Father, Son, and Holy Spirit.

The response to these things appears as stanzas to a hymn. Verses 9–10 delineate these truths: the lamb was able to take the scroll; the lamb's blood became a ransom for the nations; those ransomed became saints, a kingdom, and priests.

Verses 11–12 demonstrate that the voices of those immediately around the throne are joined by myriads and thousands of angels. The numbers are beyond counting. The Lamb is worthy of worship, ultimate allegiance in all things.

Finally, by verse 13, every creature in the creation joined the hymn. The huge chorus continued to grow and swell in magnitude—music, both text and tone, beyond our highest imaginations.

The intent of this passage was for John's original audience to be moved to a sense of worship. The contemporary reading of the passage should bring no less a response.

Genuine worship leads us to take actions that reflect the character of God as we have come to know God supremely in Jesus Christ.

We cannot expect to see visions like John. We, however, are part of the creation described in Revelation 5. Is it too much to conceive that the creation is already proclaiming the glory and praise of God? Are we too entangled in the things of life to realize it?

What we can draw from John's experience on Patmos as he observed what he described in Revelation 5 is that worship can happen anywhere and anytime for us. No matter the circumstances of our lives, God can still enter our frames of reference. The veil of mystery is parted, and for perhaps ever so briefly we can behold what God has done and is doing in this world. Maybe through large events, maybe through small ones; perhaps among a congregation of people, perhaps alone as we study the Bible and pray, or perhaps at the checkout at the grocery store—we can experience worship.

This worship forms an emotional filling and fulfilling in us. Only God can bear the weight of our need for this or respond with such peace, contentment, or wonder. This worship begins to outline and fill in what and how we are to live our lives.

One mark that one has truly worshipped is that something about God and the kingdom is more plain to us. Another mark is that having worshipped, we are never the same as we were before the time of worship. Worship is not only a lifting of the spirit, an encouragement of heart, or an enlightenment of the mind. Genuine worship leads us to take actions that reflect the character of God as we have come to know God supremely in Jesus Christ.

QUESTIONS

1. How has this study helped in your interpretation and application of the Book of Revelation?

2. What attention do you give to God's Word in your life?

3. Reflect on those places where and when you have worshipped in significant ways with God's people.

4. What experiences of worship have you had as you have beheld the magnificence of creation, such as a sunrise or sunset?

5. Plan to read Revelation 5 aloud, either alone or in the group studying this passage. What are the effects of hearing this passage in comparison to simply reading it silently?

Our Next New Study
(available for use December, 2001)

Genesis 12—50: Family Matters

Additional Resources for Studying *Genesis 12—50: Family Matters:*[1]

Walter Brueggemann. *Genesis.* Interpretation, A Bible Commentary for Teaching and Preaching. Atlanta: John Knox Press, 1982.

Bruce T. Dahlberg. "Genesis." *Mercer Commentary on the Bible.* Macon, GA: Mercer University Press, 1995.

Clyde T. Francisco. "Genesis." *Broadman Bible Commentary.* Volume 1, Revised. Nashville, Tennessee: Broadman Press, 1969.

Terence Fretheim. "The Book of Genesis." *The New Interpreter's Bible.* Volume I. Nashville: Abingdon Press, 1994.

C. T. Fritsch. *Genesis.* Layman's Bible Commentary. Volume 2. Richmond, Virginia: John Knox Press, 1959.

Victor P. Hamilton. *The Book of Genesis (Chapters 1—17).* The New International Commentary on the Old Testament. Grand Rapids, Michigan: William B. Eerdmans Publishing Company, 1990.

Victor P. Hamilton. *The Book of Genesis (Chapters 18—50).* The New International Commentary on the Old Testament. Grand Rapids, Michigan: William B. Eerdmans Publishing Company, 1995.

Derek Kidner. *Genesis: An Introduction and Commentary.* Madison, Wisconsin: InterVarsity Press, 1967.

Gordon J. Wenham. *Genesis 1—15.* Word Biblical Commentary. Volume 1. Waco, Texas: Word Books, Publisher, 1987.

Gordon J. Wenham. *Genesis 16—50.* Word Biblical Commentary. Volume 2. Waco, Texas: Word Books, Publisher, 1994.

Leon J. Wood. *Bible Study Commentary, Genesis.* Grand Rapids, Michigan: Zondervan Publishing House, 1975.

NOTES

1. Listing a book does not imply full agreement by the writers or BAPTISTWAY PRESS® with all of its comments.

How to Order More Bible Study Materials

It's easy! Just fill in the following information. Note that for *Bible Study for Texas* a Large Print edition of the *Study Guide* is available for this issue. Note also that the *Teaching Guide* for this issue includes Bible comments for teachers.

Title of item	Price	Quantity	Cost
This Issue:			
Good News in the New Testament—Study Guide	$1.95	_____	_____
Good News in the New Testament—Large Print Study Guide	$1.95	_____	_____
Good News in the New Testament—Teaching Guide	$2.45	_____	_____
Previous Issues Available:			
God's Message in the Old Testament—Study Guide	$1.95	_____	_____
God's Message in the Old Testament—Teaching Guide	$1.95	_____	_____
Matthew: Jesus As the Fulfillment of God's Promises—Study Guide	$1.95	_____	_____
Matthew: Jesus As the Fulfillment of God's Promises—Large Print Study Guide	$1.95	_____	_____
Matthew: Jesus As the Fulfillment of God's Promises—Teaching Guide	$2.45	_____	_____
Acts: Sharing God's Good News with Everyone—Study Guide	$1.95	_____	_____
Acts: Sharing God's Good News with Everyone —Teaching Guide	$1.95	_____	_____
Romans: Good News for a Troubled World—Study Guide	$1.95	_____	_____
Romans: Good News for a Troubled World—Teaching Guide	$1.95	_____	_____
Galatians: By Grace Through Faith, and Ephesians: God's Plan and Our Response—Study Guide	$1.95	_____	_____
Galatians: By Grace Through Faith, and Ephesians: God's Plan and Our Response—Large Print Study Guide	$1.95	_____	_____
Galatians: By Grace Through Faith, and Ephesians: God's Plan and Our Response—Teaching Guide	$2.45	_____	_____
Coming for use beginning December 2001			
Genesis 12—50: Family Matters—Study Guide	$1.95	_____	_____
Genesis 12—50: Family Matters—Large Print Study Guide	$1.95	_____	_____
Genesis 12—50: Family Matters—Teaching Guide	$2.45	_____	_____
Coming for use beginning March 2002			
Jesus in the Gospel of Mark—Study Guide	$1.95	_____	_____
Jesus in the Gospel of Mark—Large Print Study Guide	$1.95	_____	_____
Jesus in the Gospel of Mark—Teaching Guide	$2.45	_____	_____

Beliefs Important to Baptists

Who in the World Are Baptists, Anyway? (one lesson)	$ .45	_____	_____
Who in the World Are Baptists, Anyway?— *Teacher's Edition*	$ .55	_____	_____
Beliefs Important to Baptists: I (four lessons)	$1.35	_____	_____
Beliefs Important to Baptists: I—Teacher's Edition	$1.75	_____	_____
Beliefs Important to Baptists: II (four lessons)	$1.35	_____	_____
Beliefs Important to Baptists: II—Teacher's Edition	$1.75	_____	_____
Beliefs Important to Baptists: III (four lessons)	$1.35	_____	_____
Beliefs Important to Baptists: III—Teacher's Edition	$1.75	_____	_____

*Charges for standard shipping service:

Subtotal up to $20.00	$3.95
Subtotal $20.01—$50.00	$4.95
Subtotal $50.01—$100.00	10% of subtotal
Subtotal $100.01 and up	8% of subtotal

Please allow three weeks for standard delivery. For express shipping service: Call 1–800–355–5285 for information on additional charges.

Subtotal _____

Shipping* _____

TOTAL _____

Number of FREE copies of *Brief Basics for Texas Baptists* needed for leading adult Sunday School department periods _____

_____

Your name

_____

Your church

_____

Mailing address

_____

City   State   Zip code

MAIL this form with your check for the total amount to
Bible Study/Discipleship Center
Baptist General Convention of Texas
333 North Washington
Dallas, TX 75246–1798
(Make checks to "Baptist Executive Board.")
OR, **FAX** your order anytime to: 214–828–5187, and we will bill you.
OR, **CALL** your order toll-free: 1–800–355–5285
(8:30 a.m.–5:00 p.m., M-F), and we will bill you.
OR, **E-MAIL** your order to our internet e-mail address:
baptistway@bgct.org, and we will bill you.
We look forward to receiving your order! Thank you!